ALSO BY JACK HEINZ

FICTION

Rebellion, Love, Betrayal, 2019
Six Spies In Saranac, 2020
Engagement In Saranac, 2022
Suspicion Hardens: Two Stories, 2024

NONFICTION (PUBLISHED AS JOHN P. HEINZ)

(with A. Gordon) *Public Access to Information.* 1979
(with E. Laumann) *Chicago Lawyers, The Social Structure of the Bar.* 1982
(with E. Laumann, R. Nelson, and R. Salisbury) *The Hollow Core, Private Interests in National Policy Making.* 1993
(with R. Nelson, R. Sandefur, and E. Laumann) *Urban Lawyers, The New Social Structure of the Bar.* 2005
(with A. Heinz) *Women, Work, and Worship in Lincoln's Country, The Dumville Family Letters.* 2016

SHORT WORK

WORDS & PICTURES

SHORT WORK

WORDS & PICTURES

JACK HEINZ

DEEDS PUBLISHING

Copyright © 2025 —Jack Heinz

ALL RIGHTS RESERVED—No part of this book may be reproduced in any form or by any electronic or mechanical means, including information storage and retrieval systems, without permission in writing from the authors, except by a reviewer who may quote brief passages in a review.

Published by Deeds Publishing in Athens, GA
www.deedspublishing.com

Printed in The United States of America

Cover and interior design by Deeds Publishing

ISBN 978-1-961505-44-5

Books are available in quantity for promotional or premium use. For information, email info@deedspublishing.com.

First Edition, 2025

10 9 8 7 6 5 4 3 2 1

"My goodness, you have some wonderful material for—not a memoir, not a formal history, but some combination of the two and something else besides."

Ward Just, personal correspondence, 2011

For Otis, June, and Roxy, the future

CONTENTS

Foreword by Evan Meagher	xiii
Image: Festiniog Railway (Wales)	*xvi*
Preface	1
Image: West Main Street, Carlinville	*4*
Thanksgiving Cowboys	5
Militaria	8
Community Ties	12
Image: Quality Deer Care, Vermont	*13*
Bernadine's Photos	14
The Krupa Deprivation	19
Carlinville	22
Image: Heron Pond, near Vienna, Illinois	*27*
The Inquiring Reporter	28
The Air Force	29
Teaching	33
The Cloakroom	39
Footnotes	41
Mobility	44
Image: "He Turned Into What?"	*46*
The White House	47
The Blue House Farm	55
Etymology	57
Image: White Pines Forest, northern Illinois	*59*
Dr. Denby	60
Recitation	62
633 E. Main	64
Church	70
Image: House With Water View, Adirondacks	*73*

Flatwater Canoeing	74
The Plimpton Diversion	77
Image: Patriotic Bear, Vermont	*86*
Drosten's	87
A Proper Breakfast	90
On Not Being J. P. Donleavy	94
Image: "Just Take a Little Off the Top," Pennsylvania	*99*
Interviewed By the FBI	100
On Academic Achievement	104
Major Burke	106
The ITS	110
Image: Tree as Manet's Olympia, southern Illinois	*112*
Clothes Make the Man	113
The Chili Parlor	115
Image: Homage to Bernadine Loges, Coreys	*121*
West Main Street	122
Tea with the Landesmans	126
Stability	132
Image: Morning, After the Ball, Coreys	*135*
On Immortality	136
Image: Tom's Trunk Shop, Gabriels, NY	*139*
Leaving the Home Place	140
Walking Free	145
Image: Adirondack Knitter, Coreys	*149*
Acknowledgments	150
Image: Sunset at Coreys	*153*
Index	154

FOREWORD
BY EVAN MEAGHER

Jack Heinz has assembled a delightful assortment of short stories that depict his journey, as a child, student, writer, husband, father, and professor, giving the reader an opportunity to see the world through his evolving eyes. The narrative style mimics this variety of perspectives, with a versatility of voice that explores — among other things — his upbringing in rural Illinois, his time at the Pentagon in the early days of the Vietnam War, and his four decades teaching criminal law to first-year law students at the Northwestern Pritzker School of Law.

It was in the latter context that I first met him, when I began Northwestern's JD-MBA program in the fall of 2006, his final year of teaching. I had no interest in criminal law and, indeed, his observation about such students (in the essay titled Teaching) — "in law school only to learn about financial transactions, and to hell with criminal law until such time as they were charged with fraud or insider trading" — hits ever so slightly too close for comfort. There's a barb there, and as someone deservedly on the receiving end of it, I speak with some credibility when I say it's a good one, typical of the understated but wry humor that permeates his writing, just as it did his teaching.

I vividly recall his use of the Socratic method, and my recollection mirrors almost identically his depiction in Teaching. Even today, nearly two decades after I sat in his classroom, I can tell you with great confidence that volition was very important to White's dissent in Robinson v. California. Despite taking Crim Law (as the kids called it) for nothing more than curricular requirements, and knowing full well that my only possible exposure to the topic following law school would be as a defendant, his storytelling made an impression on me, worked its way into my imagination, and stuck there.

I expect that his storytelling will stick with you too, dear reader. The stories here speak to a sense of community, of bygone eras and simpler times: never with a sense of mawkish nostalgia, but always with a dry sense of humor and a dogged earnestness that is welcoming and endearing. His photographs have a tone consistent with his prose, suggesting not merely a sober, unflinching commitment to observing that which is real and genuine without any unnecessary pretension, but also empathy toward the subjects.

Put together, Jack's—and after two decades of "Professor Heinz," I have reluctantly agreed to call him Jack—prose and photographs speak of one man's life, career, and stories. I can only hope that you will find them as I have: a life worth living, a career worth having, and stories worth telling and reading.

Evan Meagher
Boulder, Colorado
May 2025

Festiniog Railway, Wales

PREFACE

The pieces emerged at irregular intervals, and there is no real logic to the order in which they are presented here, but there may be an inarticulate structure, as in a collage of images or a collection of found objects. The reader should feel free to dip into the collection anywhere, as I did in creating it.

The world has changed since I wrote these essays. People living then are now dead. Nature being what it is, more will be by the time you read this. But mostly I have left the texts as they were. They read better as they were written. Updating manuscripts alters not only facts but sentences, words. We all know that restaurants come and go. In a few cases, however, in which history had moved on and the change seemed important, I reluctantly revised the text. There will, of course, be references here that are unfamiliar. That is because you have had a different life than mine. In your writing, I would expect to find people and things unknown to me. I would tolerate them—or ask Siri.

The essays vary in seriousness of purpose, but only within a relatively narrow range. There's no Heidegger here and no P. G. Wodehouse or John Mortimer, more's the pity. Paul Klee's remark about "taking a line out for a walk" has been quoted by other writers who wanted you to think that they had nothing more in mind. I didn't believe them. One or two of these pieces could be read as facetious, even frivolous. But I was making fun of myself, of my habits and compulsions. There are grains of truth in them.

Why not devote the ink to the sort of thing people want? The answer is clear: what people want is appalling. Go into a Barnes & Noble (if you can still find one). The shelf labeled "Poetry" will have only a small fraction of the space devoted to "Teenage Paranormal Romance." I enjoy the act of writing, but I'm not that desperate to have an audience. I'm told that in today's fiction the characters must be "relatable." That is, readers must be able to identify with them. Really? No more Captain Ahab or Jay Gatsby? That seems a loss.

Why should Dan Brown be found in a bookstore under "literature" while A. J. Liebling is not? I recently saw E. B. White on the "classics" shelf. He died in 1985. So very long ago — halfway through my teaching career. White said, "Writing is never 'fun.'" On some days, no doubt, he really believed that. He wrote for a living, on the clock, but he almost always managed to make his work sound as if he enjoyed it. I'd like to think that he really did.

The photographs were taken during the last three

decades of the twentieth century and the first decade of this one, mostly with a folding, wooden camera that produced 4x5 inch negatives. The two earliest ones, however, were taken with a Hasselblad, which made square images, smaller. I made silver prints in my darkroom, before digital technology replaced all that. One photo was taken in Wales, one in the Midwestern town where I was born and raised, and five in the Adirondacks. The three pictures of barber shops with taxidermy came from Vermont and Pennsylvania. A mysterious, masked model appears in four of them.

J. H.
Evanston, Illinois
March, 2025

West Main Street, Carlinville

THANKSGIVING COWBOYS

"There was a Thanksgiving when the cattle got out."

"What cattle? Where?"

"They'd been in a pasture at the blue house farm, just outside town."

"I didn't know you had cows."

"Only beef cattle, not dairy cows. This was in the days before farming in central Illinois became all cash grain, all corn and soybeans. We had livestock then and fed some of our corn to the stock—cattle, hogs, a few chickens, sometimes a few sheep."

"Goats?"

"No, no goats.

"So what happened on Thanksgiving?"

"Well, we were having dinner at my grandparents' house on East Main Street and Granddad got a telephone call telling him that some of the cows were loose. This was at the blue house farm."

"The blue house farm sounds grand."

"It wasn't. It was called that because it used to have a house, painted blue. I remember it as about a two-room house, definitely not grand. By the time the cows got out, the house was gone, but the name stuck. The land was farmed by a tenant with a single-bottom plow pulled by a horse. Or maybe a mule, I'm not sure at this point. It was a long time ago. But I remember that he plowed only one furrow at a time."

"So the cows got out."

"Yeah, apparently a gate was left open, so the cows just went out in the woods. There was a creek running through and there was timber along the creek. Cows were in the woods, and Granddad said that we had to get them back in the pasture. I was maybe about twelve years old and my three Denby cousins were there, and Uncle Burke and my father, and we all went out to the farm and chased cows. We were in our good Thanksgiving clothes, but we must have been loaned boots or something."

"So you were cowboys but you didn't have horses."

"That's right. No horses. We were on foot, tramping through the woods chasing after cows."

"Did you catch them?"

"We didn't exactly catch them—we lured them. With bait. With ears of corn. When cows have been foraging in the woods, looking for nuts and berries, they get hungry and an ear of corn looks very good to them. So we were able to entice them by holding out ears of corn and getting them to walk along behind us until we were able to lead them into the pasture. I remember that Granddad got angry because he said we were giving the cows too much corn. He said we were overfeeding them. I said to him that it was Thanksgiving and everyone is overfed at Thanksgiving, so the cows might as well join in."

"That was a generous thought."

"Granddad didn't see the humor in it."

"Was it hard to do?"

"It wasn't easy because some of the cows were down by the creek, drinking water, and there were little gullies running down from the fields carrying runoff water, small streams down into the creek. Getting the cows up the steep sides of those gullies and onto level ground was a struggle."

"Did the cows follow one another in a line or did you have to round them up one by one?"

"They definitely didn't follow each other in a line. We lured them one at a time. What is the expression?—'herding cats'—herding cows is something like herding cats. My recollection is that the cows showed considerable independence."

"That must have been hard on your clothes."

"Yeah, I suppose it must have been. I don't remember much about that. I assume my mother dealt with it .... But we got the cows into the pasture"

"And closed the gate?"

"Yep, and closed the gate."

MILITARIA

In 1940, my parents took me to the Marvel Theater to see *The Howards of Virginia*, starring Cary Grant as a frontiersman who became a hero of the American Revolution. Hollywood was preparing us for war. I was four and the movie made a powerful impression. It included scenes of the suffering of Washington's army during the hard winter at Valley Forge with the soldiers' feet wrapped in rags against the cold. For the next several weeks, my feet were wrapped as I trudged through the woods next to our house.

Less than two years later the U.S. had entered World War II and my cousins and I saw the newsreels when we went to the Marvel to follow the latest exploits of Hopalong Cassidy in the serials. We saw our duty. In 1942, we were still equipped with the uniforms and weapons of the Great War. We marched on the front lawn in close order (sort of) wearing the doughboy helmets that looked like soup bowls. Also puttees. The puttees were very important, as I recall it. Photographic documentation of this ragged drill team still exists on home movies. Toward the end of the scene, we do an exaggerated rendition of exhaustion, perhaps harking back to Valley Forge. For the remainder of the war, our favorite game was a free-form affair referred to as "guns." Although the putative setting was Germany, the style of combat owed more to Tombstone.

Apart from participation in the Boy Scouts, where I learned semaphore, my military career lapsed after V-J day. In the early 1950s, however, my parents decided that I needed a dose of discipline, and they sent me to the summer program of the Culver Military Academy. (Better the summer than the full year!) My cousin had gone to Culver, as had his father. Both were in the Troop, which is the mounted cavalry, but I had greater affinity for boats, so I opted for the summer naval school.

There was a certain amount of mickey mouse at Culver, of course. We marched into the dining hall, stood at attention behind our chairs, sat upon command, "Seats!", shouted from the balcony, so that all of the 800 chairs scraped across the marble tile floor at once, with a great noise, and then we perched on the front half of our chairs. As a plebe (a boy in his first year at Culver), I was permitted to speak at table only when invited to do so by an officer (i.e., an older boy). If you committed an infraction or if the officer of the table was feeling ornery, you might be required to eat a "square meal"—your spoon or fork was required to rise from your plate in a perfectly vertical vector until it reached the approximate elevation of your mouth, where it was to make a square turn and proceed along a perfectly horizontal line until it reached your face. If it ended-up at your nose or your eye, too bad. This was all like something out of a Buster Keaton movie and it was therefore moderately amusing. The summer was, in truth, fun. There was a lot of sailing, swimming, and rowing, along with some drill that I fear resembled our front lawn in 1942. But our uniforms were better.

In the first half of the 20th century, many educational institutions emphasized the importance of good posture. There were health benefits—standing straight permitted the lungs to inflate fully and provided for the proper alignment of other organs. There was a moral element as well. One should be literally upright, "on the square." Slouching connotes sloth, indecision, defeat. At military schools, especially, posture was important. Bearing, military carriage, displayed one's fitness for leadership. An officer leading a charge should square his shoulders, the better to take the enemy's volley full in the chest.

At many colleges and prep schools, posture photos were taken to permit analysis of defects and to document improvement. In most of these photos, the victim was nude. But at Culver, mercifully, we were permitted to wear our skivvies. There were "before" and "after" photos, one taken at the beginning of the summer and the other upon departure, presumably to show that Culver had shaped us up. As I recall, the only criticism noted on my before photo was "casual head." I suppose that meant that my neck muscles were relaxed. This defect was corrected in the after version. I had pulled my chin down, thereby transforming my head from casual to, I suppose, "purposeful" or perhaps even "resolute." Given my family's records-retention policy, I think it is likely that these photos survive, filed somewhere in a cardboard box. The effect on my head, however, did not last.

COMMUNITY TIES

It was once possible to drive from town to town in the Midwest and observe that the local furniture store and the funeral home had the same family name, almost always German. German immigrants who built cabinets also made coffins. In our family, the funeral home was the responsibility of one of my uncles. One Christmas, as the family was gathering for dinner, my little brother expressed frustration about his attempts to tie his tie. Without missing a beat, Dad said: "Lie down and Uncle Harold will tie it for you."

Carlinville, Illinois, my home town, had 5800 residents in the 1870 Census and 5900 in 2010. Growth was not a high priority. For a time in the 1990s, the town had a population of 5700 according to the sign at the west city limit on Route 108, known locally as the west hard road, or 5400 if we were to believe the sign on the Shipman blacktop. Close enough.

I thought it was normal for a family to stay in the same line of work, in the same town, generation after generation. Both of my parents, all four of my grandparents, and all eight of my great-grandparents lived in Carlinville.

Quality Deer Care, Vermont

BERNADINE'S PHOTOS

In about 1930, my father's family assembled for a photo. The print I have is in the process of converting to metallic silver — I suppose it was insufficiently fixed or washed, or some such. But it was clearly taken by a professional photographer. All of the family members are seated around the table in their small dining room with a wooden box telephone mounted on the wall, and they are wearing their best clothes. The table is set with the family silver, as if for tea. The small spoons are lined up, just so. Is this all of the silver in the house, or only the best?

It looks like a stage set. It could be a scene from Eugene O'Neill. Almost Chekhov. The three sisters are there — Bernadine, Clara, and Flora, with their mother and father, and Clara's husband, Gus, and their three boys. Bernadine and Flora never married. The handsome young man in a tweed suit, slouching in his chair, one leg bent and the other stretched at full length, is my father. James Dean studied this pose.

I also have some photographs taken by Bernadine, my great aunt, probably made circa 1910 with an early Kodak. They strongly resemble, in their elan, their charm, and even their composition, those taken at about the same time by the young Jacques-Henri Lartigue. There is a celebrated Lartigue in which his brother, Zissou, is floating in a lake or pool in an inflated inner tube. In Aunt Bernadine's version, the tube is circling the body of the young man, and the half circle above him is reflected by the water, so that the circle is completed below. Like Zissou, he is not smiling or laughing but looks pensive or wistful. I don't know which photo came first, Bernadine's or Lartigue's, but I will guarantee that each proceeded independently.

Another of her pictures shows a group of six women seated in a flatbottom rowboat on the same lake. The boat appears to be dangerously overloaded. The women, of indeterminate age, perhaps ranging from thirty to fifty, are wearing long dresses with sleeves reaching their elbows — not formal gowns, but dresses suitable for church. They all have large, broad-brimmed hats of the type worn in Lartigue's pictures of the Bois de Boulogne and the Auteuil races, but without the egret feathers. The boat is broadside to the camera and the women are facing the lens, posing. It is quite formal and slightly bizarre. I think Lartigue would have liked it.

The women were probably school teachers. Bernadine taught the lower grades in the public schools of Carlinville and the surrounding area for 48 years, beginning in 1900 at the Bear Rough rural school. She was my teacher in both first grade and second grade at a time when the two grades were taught together in the same room at the old South School, which has now been converted to condos. Supervising her charges there surely sharpened her eye for what Cartier-Bresson called "the decisive moment."

Bernadine's pictures were often taken at the Macoupin Club, then and now a private refuge. The pond was created by damming a small creek in order to supply water for the steam engines of the Chicago and Alton railroad, which passed by the east shore. During my youth, a water tower stood beside the track. Water that had been pumped from the lake into the tower was siphoned into the engines. The train whistles, powered by steam, were occasionally blown for our amusement.

My Heinz grandparents owned a small cottage there, hard by the swimming area. The cottage had been wired but it had no running water or sewage system. Drinking water came from a shared well, dishwater came from the lake, and there was a rudimentary outhouse. This was all considered unremarkable at the time and place, but the color of the house was not. My grandmother visited Florida in 1950 and was, regrettably, impressed by the bright pink houses she saw there. The paint, called "Shocking Pink," caused a stir at the Macoupin Club.

The swimming area had a dock with a wooden diving board on the end, and a raft. On either side of the dock were sheds designated as dressing rooms. The one for men housed a large mud dauber nest, with active wasp traffic. The nest was there every year. This encouraged rapid and alert disrobing.

The raft was made of heavy timbers without any oil drums or other flotation device. It rode low in the water. When you tried to climb onto it, your side would sink, so that you could almost swim on. This presented opportunities for mischief. If we saw a swimmer approaching the raft, we would all immediately move to the opposite side, with the result that our side would sink and the swimmer was confronted with a goal that was now three feet up in the air. Because the raft was slippery, however, it was also easy to jettison those on the submerged side, and this was often an attractive option, so that the raft would then tend to level and achieve an equilibrium state.

The pond was created by an earthen dam. The area below the dam, where the old streambed continued to carry the overflow from the small spillway, was dark and damp. It was heavily populated with snakes and was called "Snake Hollow." In the hot weather, snakes sunned themselves on the top of the dam. To get from our cottage to the picnic and playground area, it was necessary either to cross the dam or to walk a much more circuitous route along the road. We took the short way. In summer, we chose our footfalls carefully and stepped over a good many snakes.

The pond supported a considerable bloom of duckweed, and the prevailing wind concentrated the duckweed at the swimming area. The water was often carpeted with green. A swimmer emerging from the water tended to resemble the gargoyle in an aquatic garden. This contributed to the popularity of the breaststroke, especially a version with a broad sweeping motion.

The governing committee of the club spread large amounts of copper sulfate each spring in an effort to control the duckweed. (It is clear that the persistence of the mud daubers in the dressing shed was not attributable to environmental sensitivities.) Copper sulfate, also known as blue vitriol, is quite poisonous. It had no noticeable effect on the duckweed, and the health of the swimmers was not monitored. Better dead than green. In more recent years, the club has introduced a family of ducks, who eat the duckweed. Who knew?

THE KRUPA DEPRIVATION

My body is equipped with an odd assortment of bone structure. I have strong legs, as did my father, and strangely short fingers of obscure origin. From my mother's side, the Denbys, I inherited the classic British weak lower jaw. I am a chinless wonder, but without the money or title to go with it. I grew a beard in an attempt to conceal this — it is not entirely successful, of course. When I was young, my parents sought to compensate for heredity through orthodontia and I was subjected to years of braces, rubber bands that were supposed to pull my lower jaw forward, and other torture devices. This meant that any basketball or football game was sure to result in lacerations of my mouth that left me spitting blood. The braces did not create a chin.

When I was about 13, the orthodontist paid the expenses for my parents to take me to Chicago, so that I could be shown. Perhaps I was an example of an especially horrible case, material for a cautionary tale. It is implausible that I could have been regarded as a success story. But I was told that my orthodontist was seeking elevation to a higher level of distinction—perhaps an O.B.E. (Over Bite Eradicator) or maybe even a K.C.B. (Knight Commander of Buckteeth). In any event, I was displayed and inspected.

We were put up at the Hotel Sherman, in the Loop. It was nice enough. The Sherman had a thriving nightclub, the College Inn, which booked big name music. At the time of our small contribution to science, the Gene Krupa big band was appearing there. Krupa was at the height of his fame. He had become a star in Benny Goodman's band in the 1930s—his solo on "Sing Sing Sing" at the 1938 Carnegie Hall concert caused a sensation. The Gene Krupa Story, a technicolor biopic starring Sal Mineo in the title role, was yet to come (1959), but the Krupa band at the College Inn was a hard-driving, high-energy show. It used arrangements by a young Gerry Mulligan, and it had Don Fagerquist and Red Rodney, a Charlie Parker protege, on trumpets and Frank Rosolino on trombone. These were all great players.

I wanted to see the show. My parents wouldn't let me. I hung around the doorway of the club for a few minutes and heard some of it. But not enough. My parents vetoed Krupa because he had been busted for marijuana use and jailed for 84 days. He was, they thought, not a proper role model. (Though my parents didn't know it, at least not at the time, Red Rodney was a Parker protege in drugs that were far more destructive than marijuana, Mulligan had his own drug problems, and Rosolino met a sad and violent end.) I would like to think that my parents' caution was well-founded, but I fear that my capacity for rebellion was (and is) distinctly limited. Anyone who spends 42 years in the same job, teaching about rules, deserves a high score on the stability scale. It's true that I played drums in a high school jazz band, but I was never any more likely to match Krupa's lifestyle than I was to equal his speed and skill.

Years later, I fell and hit my mouth on a large rock. I knocked out a couple of teeth and a piece of bone in my upper jaw. When the maxillofacial surgeon told me that he intended to graft a piece of my lower jaw into the upper to provide support for prosthetic teeth, I protested that I didn't have much lower jaw to spare. This stimulated a conversation about orthodontia (but not about Krupa). He said, "Nowadays we would just break your lower jaw and move it forward." I think I prefer the beard.

CARLINVILLE

When our son, Peter, was about eight or nine years old, I explained to him that he was from Carlinville. He replied: "Dad, we live in Evanston." That was true enough, but I pointed out that, although I had then lived in Evanston for three decades, I was born in Carlinville, went to the public schools there, and consistently said (even without being asked), "I'm from Carlinville." That didn't work with Peter. He knew where he was born: "Yeah, but I was born in Evanston." Ah. True again, but I said, "A mere accident of birth. Suppose, say, you were born in a car while we were passing through Nilwood en route from Springfield to Carlinville. Then you would surely still be from Carlinville. Or, suppose I was in the Foreign Service and you were born in, say, Paris, you would still be an American, not a Frenchman. You are from Carlinville by inheritance, the *jus sanguinas*." He looked at me strangely.

Approaching Carlinville, the first thing you see is the courthouse dome. It is a fitting symbol of the power of the law, but it was purchased dear. Construction was budgeted at $175,000. The final cost, in 1870, was $1,340,000, serious money in the 19th Century, thus demonstrating not only the majesty of the law but the entrepreneurial opportunities that it presents. The building is in the Second Empire style, more or less, and is clad in yellow limestone. Originally, even the sidewalks were limestone. Those wore out. The main doors are cast iron, and each weighs more than a ton. They still open and close. The inside stairways are also iron, and the newel posts at the bottom are cast pelicans. So far as I know, no pelican has ever been sighted in Macoupin County except in the courthouse. The grounds were once surrounded by a decorative iron fence, but this was sacrificed for a scrap metal drive in one of the World Wars, a home front campaign that was, I'm told, designed more for civilian morale than for military success. I have no memory of the fence, but I've seen pictures of it and I regret the loss.

An Amtrak passenger arriving in Carlinville from the north will see the county fairgrounds on the left, with a track and grandstand used for harness races. At the city limits, a large fleet of the refrigerated trucks of the Prairie Farms Creamery is prominent on the right, and the train then travels a dozen blocks past small, modest houses before reaching the center of town. Large grain elevators stand next to the tracks, north of the West Main Street crossing. The station is just beyond it, so that stopped trains block the crossing. All of this is reassuring in its familiarity. The landmarks have not changed in decades.

As soon as a town gets money, it starts tearing things down and building new. In Carlinville, historic preservation has been popular, of necessity. There are, however, some new houses around the edges, often outside the city limits. A Walmart was built on what was once a commercial iris field. As in many other towns, the businesses on the city square could not compete and many closed. A picture of Carlinville's square published in *Life* during World War II is still recognizable as the same place, but there is more traffic in the old picture.

Although a lack of capital has slowed change in the appearance of the town, the social structure is now quite different. People not born in Carlinville and who have no antecedents there occupy prominent places in the society. Of course, the balance sheet also determines much of this. The new class is in residence there just as surely as in the high-rise apartments on Chicago's Lake Shore Drive, but more modestly. Entrepreneurs have largely (but not completely) displaced landed gentry.

Because of the scale of the town, the different social classes see each other more often than they do in cities. Proximity matters. I would bet that marriage between persons of differing standing, while relatively unlikely, is more probable in Carlinville than in Chicago. Carlinville has only one high school, and only three grade schools. There are no private schools. Race is not a factor. There are a few Black families in town, but not enough to be regarded as a constituency. So far as I can see, race doesn't correlate with social class. The numbers are too small. When my mother went to the Carlinville schools in the early twentieth century, she had two Black classmates. I had none.

Importantly, perhaps, residents who were raised in Carlinville continue to see classmates for the rest of their lives, in the grocery store and at the gas station. There is no Whole Foods; there is no Starbucks. If you eat out, you have a choice of Taylor's Chili Parlor, in an alley off the town square, The Glades, a roadhouse across from the Carlin-Villa Motel, Reno's pizza and spaghetti, on the north side of the square, Angus Bailey's steak house, near Reno's, Nick's pizza and spaghetti out by the old Walmart, or Magnolias, a ladies' luncheon place. Your classmates will see you there. You know what has become of them and they know about you, without Facebook. This imposes a powerful discipline. It is probably one of the reasons for the popularity of cities.

One of my uncles said that he stayed in Carlinville because he wanted to be a big fish in a small pond. Maybe that was a rational choice. Maybe he had a real opportunity to go elsewhere and decided against it. But I doubt that most of us are able to be so calculating in plotting a strategy for the life course. Instead, one thing just seems to lead naturally to another. At some point we get married, children are born, parents grow old, get sick, die. You and I are not truly free to join the Abraham Lincoln Brigade; not for long.

Heron Pond, near Vienna, Illinois

THE INQUIRING REPORTER

When I was in high school, the inquiring reporter for the school newspaper asked me the question of the week, "What is your pet peeve?" I said, "hypocrites." A reasonable response, but commonplace. Fortunately, however, the reporter was a poor speller. When my answer appeared in the paper, it was rendered as "Hippocrites." This was taken by many to mean "Hippocrates," which was certainly as reasonable a reading as any.

Being peeved with Hippocrates would have been expected if we had been assigned any reading about the Greeks, but this was Macoupin County, Illinois, in the early 1950s. We were not burdened with trivia, and the revelation that Hippocrates was my pet peeve was greeted with awe. Hey, my colleagues said, this is pretty heavy stuff. My career was launched.

THE AIR FORCE

In the early 1960s, men were eligible for the draft until the age of 26. If you could manage to be "deferred" until you reached that age, you had escaped, and I was only three months short of 26 when I completed law school and my student exemption expired. Deferments were mostly within the discretion of local draft boards composed of people in your home town (referred to in a government report as "little groups of neighbors"). As I approached graduation, many of my classmates obtained continuing deferments, either to clerk for a federal judge or to teach. Those men came from big cities. But my draft board said, in effect, that I would be conscripted if I did not "volunteer." The board drew on a rural area. If young men from the farms were to be drafted, depriving their families of their labor, the Carlinville board felt that smartass graduates of the Yale Law School should also serve. This was tolerably just, even I had to admit. The Vietnam war had not yet made military service dangerous—we didn't fear the draft then, we merely resented the fact that it delayed the start of our careers.

Luckily, the office of the general counsel of the

Air Force came to Yale looking for people with draft boards like mine. They offered me a commission as an officer for three years of legal work in the Pentagon, in the office of the Secretary of the Air Force, in civilian clothes. Thus, I had the choice of spending three years as an officer in mufti or being drafted and serving two years as an enlisted man, God knows where. I took the commission.

A part of the mythology of the Pentagon is that there is civilian control of the military. Since the service Secretarys are prime symbols of this control, it was important to maintain the appearance of a civilian office, and my fellow officers and I were therefore instructed (maybe "ordered" is the correct word) to dress in ordinary business suits. For the first year and a half that I worked there, I didn't even own a uniform. In truth, the masking of the military presence in the office was not a substantial misrepresentation, at least so far as we were concerned. We were civilians through and through.

There was also an operational reason for our status to be concealed. In the nature of our work, it was sometimes necessary for us to tell military commanders that they could not do as they wished. This message, delivered by a first lieutenant to a colonel, would not have gone down well. Many of the senior officers we dealt with must have known what we were, the informal channels of communication within the Pentagon being at least as efficient as the formal ones, but it would have created awkwardness if they had admitted that they knew. It was better to play dumb. ("If you want to get along, go along." Sam Rayburn.) Once, when I visited an Air Force base, I was assigned a driver and a staff car with one star on the plate, signifying a brigadier general or a civilian of equivalent rank. In retrospect, this seems outrageous.

Given today's security concerns, it is difficult to imagine the lack of protection of the Pentagon then. Anyone could enter without showing identification. A public bus line had a regular stop in the basement of the building alongside a shopping concourse, and from there most of the Pentagon was freely accessible through unguarded corridors. A bus could, of course, carry thousands of pounds of explosives. Only a few parts of the building had restricted access when I worked there. There was, however, secret business taking place and my job required a "top secret" clearance. This was routine for people working in the office of the Secretary.

During the Cuban missile crisis, however, we had a sense of our vulnerability. Intelligence reports indicated that missiles were targeted at the Pentagon, and we were told that all officers were to be issued sidearms. How this would have defended us against a missile is not entirely clear. Probably, the fear was that the missile attack would be followed by widespread panic or perhaps even by an invasion. Fortunately, the journalist John Scali's backchannel meetings at the Occidental restaurant with Soviet go-betweens bore fruit before the pistols were distributed. The danger to life and limb if my friends and I had guns would have been real.

TEACHING

The professor enters the room carrying the "casebook", a compilation of judicial opinions. It is the first day in law school for the seventy-five students. They have not seen the professor before, but they know his name. A posted notice had told them to read Robinson vs. California. The professor goes immediately to the bare lectern and removes from his jacket a list of student names. He looks up at the students.

His first words are, "Mr. Culpeper, tell us please about Robinson against California."

Culpeper is stunned but game. He begins to describe a decision of the U. S. Supreme Court. Then, as soon as he says something interesting or problematic, the professor interrupts:

"Mr. Culpeper, you said that the police officer examined Robinson's arms and found needle tracks. Where did that examination take place?"

Answer: "On the street."

"Can police officers just stop anyone on the street and tell them to roll up their sleeves? 'Don't move! I want to examine your arms!'"

Answer: "The Supreme Court's decision says 'Officer Brown testified that he had occasion to examine the appellant's arms one evening on a street in Los Angeles.'"

"What sort of occasion is that? An arm-examining occasion? Had Robinson done something wrong, or was there reason to be suspicious of him?"

Answer: "Well, if the officer stopped him, I suppose there must have been some reason to be suspicious of him."

"Does the officer need to have any basis for that suspicion?"

Answer: "Like what?"

"Like, maybe, cause to believe that a crime had been committed."

An issue, once raised, is often left unresolved. Sometimes this is done because the courts have not articulated a clear rule, and sometimes the teacher simply wants to motivate the students to be curious, think about it, and perhaps do some research on their own.

It is a large room with dark brown woodwork and stained glass windows, an old-fashioned lecture hall, two stories tall. The students are seated in steeply-raked rows arranged in a U shape so that those in the two arms of the U face each other across the well of the house. The professor can move at will. If he is talking with a student seated near the lectern at the lower level, it will be necessary for him to climb to the top of the U so that students in the nether reaches will be able to hear the conversation. The professor had damn-well-better be in good shape, have good legs.

I didn't introduce myself. They knew who I was. The class simply starts by going through the case. This was intended to make the point that law school was serious business. No nonsense, no chit-chat. I tried to make my teaching precise, disciplined, demanding. I wanted them to become good lawyers. They wanted that too, and it was my job to help them develop the skills.

There is a "law professor manner." It is an occupational affliction. We tend to press the issue, even in ordinary conversations. Some might see this as being analytical, which is how we tend to see ourselves. Others, however, might characterize it as merely obnoxious. For me, the most difficult thing about being a law professor was striking the right balance between friendliness and aggressiveness. I didn't want to be a tyrant—in truth, I actually wanted the students to like me—but I knew that I did them no favor if I gave them an easy pass. They needed to learn. One of the things that made this difficult was the individual differences among students. In a large class, you have the full range—some were confident, eager to talk, and some were timid, silent. I had to teach both, at the same time. And they had differing objectives.

Some were intellectuals and were engaged by intellectual problems; others were in law school only to learn about financial transactions, and to hell with criminal law until such time as they were charged with fraud or insider trading.

Some professors call on volunteers—of whom, regrettably, there are always far too many. In those classes, students who chose the law as an outlet for their aggressive impulses dominate the proceedings, to the great annoyance of their fellows.

I started teaching in August of 1965, just after I completed my Air Force tour of duty. The Vietnam war was then in its early stages, and the anti-war protests were beginning to get organized. It was a volatile, politically charged time to be teaching criminal law. Malcolm X was assassinated in 1965. The Selma march was also that year. The assassinations of Martin Luther King and Robert Kennedy took place during the first half of 1968, before the tumultuous Democratic National Convention in Chicago. Police conduct became a hot, divisive issue. I'm not sure whether the students knew that I had worked in the Pentagon—I don't recall encountering hostility.

I tried to be impartial. Effective teaching of law requires an ability to argue either side of a case. Some arguments were, of course, better than others, but regardless of the position a student took it was my duty to make him (in those days, it was still usually him) defend his position. A good lawyer needed to see the counter-argument, to anticipate it in order to defeat it and to see the weaknesses in his own case. This is probably why lawyers are so often perceived to be unprincipled. The job of the professional advocate is sometimes a difficult one and, depending upon one's view of ethical obligations, it can be uncomfortable. A colleague and I did the post-conviction appeals for a man who committed murder while out on parole after having served a long sentence for a previous murder. He was under sentence of death. For a long time, I received Christmas cards from him.

When I started teaching, there were a few women in my classes, but only a few. The seating charts in those days included only last names. The few women had "Ms" in front of the name, which was useful for the professor's orientation. The chart showed that Martin could be found next to the woman, and Radzinowicz was two seats higher up than the woman. But when the number of women in law schools increased, women were no longer useful landmarks. The entry of women into the legal profession in large numbers began in about 1970, when only 2.8 percent of U. S. lawyers were women. By 1988, nearly 40 percent of law school graduates were women.

In my early years in teaching, I was young and loose (or maybe flippant). I didn't know what I was doing, and that didn't bother me. In the middle of my career, however, the performance part of teaching annoyed me. I had become more knowledgeable, and I deeply cared. It offended me if it seemed that a student did not. I pushed. Some students resented the pushing and I resented their resentment. In my old age, I relaxed again. I found that I couldn't really force them to learn and that a more humane approach, with less pressure, less angst, might be conducive to learning. I slowed down. It probably prolonged my career.

THE CLOAKROOM

At my grade school, the walk-in closet where we put our coats was referred to as "the cloakroom." Not the "coat room," the cloakroom. I spent a fair amount of time there because it was where the deportment problems were incarcerated. Perhaps being in the presence of empty coats was meant to suggest transience, and thus to encourage penitence. It was a bit like transportation to Australia—a form of isolation or banishment, the equivalent of "the cooler" in this stalag, but none of us yet had the example of Steve McQueen and his baseball.

One day were all instructed by our teacher to make a noise, one at a time, with some object that we had brought to school for that purpose. Other members of the class were to close their eyes and guess what had produced the sound. As usual, I forgot about the assignment, and so I brought nothing. When my turn came, I got up and went to the back of the classroom where there was a water faucet. I drew a glass of water and gargled. Naturally enough, the other students immediately identified the source of the sound—the teacher, however, accused them of peeking because I had gargled up the scale, which the teacher found impressive. It is hard to imagine what else that sound might have been, but perhaps the teacher admired my creativity, or my nerve. In any event, I was spared another visit to the cloakroom.

How long had it been since the students in Carlinville wore cloaks? I am told that in England schools still have cloakrooms. Even more remarkably, the anteroom outside the chamber of the U.S. Senate is known as the cloakroom. Tradition and continuity, by God! Cloakrooms have survived at least a century longer than cloaks, not because wood and nails are more durable than cloth, but because language is durable. New words are added, but old ones are slow to die.

We change our prattle, of course, ("neologism" is an invention begat by invention), but we don't clean out the lexicon as often as we clean old clothes out of the closet (or cloakroom). We need a resale store for archaic words. Some of us, of course, when inserting a CD into the player, say that we are going to listen to the Victrola. It is this inclination that explains both the Senate and the English.

FOOTNOTES

In the early years of my academic career, there was little pressure to do research or scholarly writing. Law professors were primarily lawyers. But there was something known as "the tenure piece," an article (singular) demonstrating ability to do scholarly work. The article almost always appeared in a law review, weighed down with literally hundreds of footnotes.

After the tenure piece, some law professors chose to feather their oars. They settled into a quiet, restful life, doing a bit of consulting, a bit of public service, and perhaps some speaking. This idyll was interrupted twice a year by the excruciating tedium of reading blue books (exams), but otherwise it was a gig where the audience was required to applaud. What could be better?

This left plenty of time for the pursuit of passing fancies. Lacking a talent for marital infidelity, I began work on an article about boxing. Benny Paret and Davey Moore had been killed in the ring, and allegations of underworld connections had surfaced once again. Abolitionists were on the move, so I titled the piece "In Defense of the Sweet Science." But the real impetus for writing it was the death of A.J. Liebling. I had encountered Liebling's masterpiece, *The Sweet Science*, in the Linonia and Brothers room at the Yale library—a room to which women were not, then, granted admittance, not from concern that the books found there would corrupt them or offend their refined sensibilities, but simply from sheer meanness. This was a part of Yale's program of education for life … in the Union League Club. In any event, with few compunctions, I went in, pulled Liebling from the shelf, and settled in a splendid, overstuffed, leather-upholstered club chair, where I remained for hours, entranced by Liebling's account of Archie Moore as Ahab and Pierce Egan as Herodotus.

When Liebling died, I felt I owed him something. He had kept me away from the doctrine of worthier title. I had reason to be grateful. My boxing article was intended as a tribute, and I consciously emulated some of his mannerisms. He often, for example, made playful use of similes and analogies, the more outrageous the better. In a footnote to the word "probably," therefore, I wrote: "Probably is to a journalist what a protective cup is to a boxer. If he is attacked for the statement, the journalist can clutch his qualifier and groan that he was fouled." It is significant that this was in a footnote. My article was the first that *Sports Illustrated* published with footnotes.

As the manuscript was making its way through

the editorial process at SI, an editor contacted me with the news that the footnotes would have to go. (There were 14 of them.) I replied that the footnotes couldn't go; they were an integral part of the essay. But, she said, you don't understand, SI doesn't even have a typeface or a layout for footnotes. I allowed as how, with the resources of Time Inc., they could solve that problem. They did.

John Fowles wrote a letter to SI saying that he liked my article. As a result, SI invited him to write about cricket. His article became the second SI piece that used footnotes.

MOBILITY

In the Carlinville of the 1950s, it mattered that a family had been there for a century. Your ancestors need not have accomplished much, but it was important that they had been there, not elsewhere. Achievement, after all, is transitory, but family, barring exile or infertility, endures. The value of a successful career as a concert pianist paled beside the accomplishment of owning land for five generations. There was practicality in this—if your hands became arthritic, you would still have the land.

On both the German side (Heinz and Loges) and the British side (Denby and Burke), relatives abounded. It would have been hard to avoid them, not that one tried. Lineage was the favorite topic of conversation at the Denby dinner table, not so much as an exercise in snobbery (though there was certainly an element of that) as a feat of recollection. Any family of the vicinity might be traced back to the point at which it appeared in Macoupin County. The conversation should have been transcribed for a PhD dissertation on social networks and courtship patterns.

The members of my family who came of age before World War II married within the community and stayed there. Given the limited breeding stock available in a town with a few thousand people, the marriage of my mother and father was not the first between their families, with the result that I am my own cousin, at some appropriately distant remove. Later cohorts looked elsewhere.

There were not many opportunities for social mobility. The local culture and the local economy combined to make advancement or decline unlikely. Although sin would become immediately known to all, it had to be pretty dramatic to make a real difference, and the town did not provide much scope for the demonstration of skill as an artist, real estate developer, or community organizer. To strut upon the stage, one needed to leave. The people who were not interested in strutting, and stayed put, were sometimes much nicer (but not always).

He Turned Into What?

THE WHITE HOUSE

I worked in the Pentagon during the McNamara years. He had a reputation for arrogance, but he was, in one respect at least, quite democratic. I lifted weights and jumped rope at the Pentagon Officers Athletic Club ("the POAC"), and the shower room was often crowded. One day I was aware of a man standing behind me, waiting for my shower. I took my time. When I washed the soap out of my eyes and turned around, I saw that it was Robert McNamara, wearing the Secretary's new clothes. I thought that was commendable; no doubt he had other options.

After about a year and a half I was promoted to the rank of captain (this was standard), and shortly thereafter I was selected for additional duty as a "social aide" at the White House. This meant that I had to dress up in fancy uniforms and attend social events, including state dinners and receptions. I often worked at the Pentagon during the day and at the White House at night, but there were daytime events as well. We were told that, since the President and the First Lady could not be everywhere at once, we were to serve as hosts. Mostly, this meant that we helped people find their way around, and we danced with some of the guests (only females). The ten aides were all male, all officers, and all unmarried. When I explained the assignment to my mother, she said: "I see. You're sort of a costumed gigolo." Although I had worn glasses for years, I was required to wear contact lenses while on duty at the WH. The social aides were all about appearance. We did not deliver food or drinks, and we were not an honor guard. They had waiters for the former and enlisted men for the latter. It became clear to me that our purpose was primarily decorative.

The uniforms were definitely cool. In addition to several varieties of dress uniforms, depending upon the occasion and the time of year, we all wore aiguillettes (defined in my *Webster's Collegiate* as "a shoulder cord worn by a high military aide"). Worn on the right shoulder, as ours were, it indicated that the officer was an aide to the head of state. These were made of gold or silver braid, depending upon your service. The overall effect was festive, rather like tinsel on a Christmas tree. The uniforms were, in a real sense, what it was all about. We reinforced "Hail to the Chief."

When I was selected for the White House assignment, my first problem was to acquire the necessary costumes. I had none of them. My second problem was to learn how to wear them. I had to look at a book to figure out where the various pieces of insignia belonged. At substantial personal expense, I bought all of the uniforms up to and including the black tie version, with both black and white jackets (winter and summer). We wore them all. As the 1964 presidential election and the 1965 inauguration approached, I was told that I would need the white tie and tails uniform because the inaugural balls always required white tie. I had to be prepared, and white tie was not standard Air Force issue. But that uniform is (or was) simply a civilian white tie and tails with silver buttons and the insignia of one's rank sewn onto the lower sleeve. So I got measured and suitably equipped. About a month or so before the inauguration, we were told that Lyndon Johnson, being a Texan, had decided to break with tradition. The inaugural balls would be black tie. But I did get to wear the damn thing once, at a formal ball given by the diplomatic corps. Now, by changing the buttons and removing the insignia, I would still be suitably equipped should I ever be invited to do a rendition of "Puttin' on the Ritz" (like Peter Boyle in *Young Frankenstein*).

During the inaugural festivities, my principal duty was to escort the President's aunt and uncle, Mr. and Mrs. Huffman Baines, who were very pleasant. We were assigned a staff car and driver, but since Mr. Baines was old and could not walk far, I had to persuade numerous police to allow us to drive through checkpoints and around barriers intended to keep even official cars at a distance. This required some creativity. On our way to the inauguration at the east steps of the Capitol, I managed to get to a side door, and then escorted them to the dais by the shortest route. As we came out of a hallway, I saw TV cameras directly in front of us. Because the networks were expecting the President and First Lady to appear at that point, the Baineses and I appeared onscreen. Back home in Carlinville, the guys at the Heinz Furniture store were watching the proceedings. The reporter said: "We don't know who this is." Scrappy Fite replied to the TV: "We do. It's Jack."

Mr. and Mrs. Baines were seated down in front, under the canopy, near the Johnsons and the podium. I waited up the steps in the Capitol. Partway through the ceremony, I received a message that Mr. Baines was feeling ill and that I should escort him out. This required me to descend the stairs on the main aisle, go to his chair, help him to his feet, and then support him as we slowly mounted the stairs to re-enter the Capitol. I had my eyes on Mr. Baines, but when we reached the top of the stairs I came face to face with the Joint Chiefs, all four of them, just a few feet away. I wished that I had learned how to salute—but, to do so, I would have had to drop Mr. Baines.

After delivering him to the physician's office in the Capitol, I returned to my post, the waiting area.

A short time later, I was instructed by the WH to go back down the steps to tell Mrs. Baines that her husband was none the worse, and then stay with her, sitting in his chair, to keep her company. This required me to go by the Joint Chiefs again and, since my hands were not encumbered this time, I might actually need to salute. This could have been awkward. So I contrived to approach them from the rear, stealthily, so that they couldn't see me until I was already in the clear, with my back to them.

I ended up seated for the inaugural oath of both the President and the Vice-President, well in front of many senior government officials, and considerably in front of the Joint Chiefs. The next day, my picture appeared on the front page of the *Washington Post*—along with the other dignitaries, of course.

The Baineses were staying at the Blair House, just across the street from the WH. The woman in charge of Blair House, Mrs. Wilroy, wrote an account of her time there entitled *Inside Blair House*. In the book, she credits me with carrying Mr. Baines up the stairs to his room. It never happened. I think it is likely that one of the other aides carried him up at a time when I was not present, but her notes told her that I was the officer assigned to look after him. An understandable error. I point this out for the benefit of future historians.

Although the inauguration was interesting, it was

not the high point of my time at the WH. That was clearly the Festival of the Arts. It had been planned during the Kennedy administration, primarily by Arthur Schlesinger, Jr., I believe, but it was not held until after the assassination. It was truly an extraordinary assembly of talent and was designed to permit the artists to wander about, talking to each other. I was also permitted to wander and talk. I met Man Ray and Edward Steichen (Captain, USN, and don't you forget it!). Man Ray was a nice guy, very friendly, unassuming. Steichen, then 86, was gruff, quite haughty, and had his beautiful young wife with him. With something to live for, he lasted another eight years. I talked with Jason Robards about his reading of Fitzgerald's "The Crack-Up", on television. He told me that he did it as atonement for the awful movie version of *Tender is the Night*, in which he co-starred with Jill St. John. Robards was then married to Lauren Bacall (Betty) and he did an imitation of her imitating Jill St. John. Lee J. Cobb and Mildred Dunnock performed a scene from *Death of a Salesman* in the East Room, before an audience of 35 to 50 — not on a stage, just with guests gathered around them. Cary Grant commented on the crop dusting scene from *North by Northwest*. Duke Ellington and his orchestra performed on the lawn on a stage raised only a few feet. I stood next to the stage, just in front of Johnny Hodges. Beyond category!

Dwight Macdonald, the literary critic and general troublemaker, was also there. A few years before, I had read his *Memoirs of a Revolutionist*. I told him that I liked it. He looked at me strangely and said, "Oh, you read that, did you?", in an accusatory tone. Here was a young man in military uniform saying that he admired a left-wing essay. In Macdonald's world, this did not compute. He probably thought I was a red-chaser in military intelligence. A week later, he published a piece in the *New York Review of Books* that commented on the "crisp, incredibly clean white uniform accented only by brass buttons, silver shoulder-bars and one of those military shoulder corsages of gold cords and tassels looped over the left shoulder." (It was the right shoulder, but never mind.)

In three years of active duty, I had no encounter with violence of any kind, not even in the hallways or parking lots of the Pentagon. The Vietnam war had started, but it had not yet escalated. Some, however, already saw the disaster that it would become. Robert Lowell refused, on principle, to come to the Festival of the Arts. John Hersey came but chose to read from his *Hiroshima*.

I wish I had had the wit to extract something profound or even colorful from these conversations — the one with Man Ray, especially, something about the birth of Dada, about Paris in the twenties, or about Kiki or Lee Miller. But I was just being friendly and so was he. He was easy-going, unassuming, no big deal, Brooklyn still in his voice. The Festival of the Arts had delivered him to me. He was standing beside me and willing to talk, but I lacked sophistication and ideas and I failed to take full advantage of the opportunity.

My military service was entirely as a non-combatant, but the seriousness of the larger enterprise was clear to me. It became even clearer. My best friend among the WH aides was a navy pilot, Bill Coakley, who happened to be the younger brother of one of the lawyers in my Pentagon office. A few months later, Bill's plane, having been hit by a missile, crashed on a mountain in Vietnam. His name is on the memorial near the reflecting basin.

THE BLUE HOUSE FARM

No Ibbetsons have lived in the Ibbetson house for half a century, and Daisy Minton's house is still hers despite her death in 1935. The Messick house remains the Messick house even though a boy who grew up there after the Messicks had long departed became an actor and got his picture in *The New Yorker!* All place names are historical.

The Blue House farm has had no house since 1950, and the blue paint fell off long before that. In the early years of World War II, however, tenants still lived there and tilled the ground. James Bryan, his wife, Josephine, and their dog, Speck, occupied the two rooms. There was also a fruit (or root, or storm) cellar dug into the rise of land behind the house. The ruins of the cellar and of a smokehouse are still visible. Little else is.

James Bryan was small, wiry, weathered, soft spoken. He made his furrows with a horse-drawn plow, one row at a time. This was fortunate for me because, as he walked behind the plow, he was able to see the arrowheads that were turned up, and I got some of them. My cousins got the others. The Bryans had no children, and he may well have thought that the arrowheads belonged to the landowner. I doubt that he was aware of the labor theory of value.

He was, however, an educated man. He could read and write—his handwriting was, in fact, quite precise, almost elegant (a concept not well-understood in the computer age). This fact made some people suspicious. They thought he was "educated beyond his station—he must be hiding something." I knew this was nonsense. He was a very nice man, and he was a source of arrowheads. No doubt he had led a tough life, but no one seemed to know where, or anything else about his history. That didn't stop the speculation, of course.

His wife appeared to have come from different circumstances. She didn't read or write. She wore her hair in a bowl cut—quite literally, cut with the aid of a bowl, I think—and she was a head taller than he. Her speech fell somewhere between an accent and a defect. When trying to quiet their dog, Speck, she would say: "Peck, be quite or I'll shane you to a share." She was pleasant (even to Speck, most of the time), but she seemed to be hewn from rougher stuff. There were even those who suggested that James and Josephine were not really married. I never heard any evidence cited on the proposition, one way or the other.

ETYMOLOGY

The recent controversy about the Regional Transit Authority brought to mind my first annoyance with public transportation. It was not that I had trouble getting from one place to another—in about fifteen minutes, you could walk across the town where I grew up. Rather, the difficulty came in my grade school arithmetic class. When I was ten, most of the "word problems" had to do with budgets, and all of those budgets included an allowance for "carfare." I had no idea what that was. There were plenty of cars in town, but none of them charged fares. No taxis. And there were no streetcars—in fact no public transportation of any kind. At first, I read the word as "carefare," an etymological cousin of "carefree" that I invented for the purpose of interpreting those budgets. In my mind, carefare was the rough equivalent of "entertainment," an item in which the textbook budgets were always woefully deficient.

The most popular entertainment in that town was and is eating. This may have been predestined by the name of the place. The county is called Macoupin, which is said to be the name in some American Indian language for an edible tuber, akin to the potato. It bode well for my future as a feeder to have spent my formative years in a place dedicated to a food, especially one of such seriousness as the potato. Too few counties are named after vegetables.

White Pines Forest, northern Illinois

DR. DENBY

About a week after my grandfather Denby died, my grandmother and I walked into the front hall and saw his old, battered hat on the sideboard. She stopped short and said: "It's remarkable how much a hat can look like a man."

He had not seemed especially old or battered, even to my 13-year old eyes, but the hat clearly captured a part of him. It was the one he wore when he slopped the hogs. He had varied pursuits—he was a doctor transformed into a bank president, and he fed the livestock. He practiced medicine until his early fifties, when he heeded a call to run the small, local bank in which his family owned the controlling interest, and he then did that job for twenty-six years, until his death.

He was in charge of the bank during the Depression. My mother remembered him sitting in the living room of the Main Street house listening to the radio as he wept with relief after the announcement that FDR had declared the Bank Holiday, closing all of the banks temporarily to prevent runs on them. Before that day, Granddad had been a Republican, but he was a Democrat for the remainder of his life. The Farmers' & Merchants' Bank of Carlinville was found to be sound, and it reopened. Many did not.

He was a man of average height and weight, bald, with a fringe of white hair around the edges, clean-shaven, dignified, thoughtful, precise. He dressed conservatively, usually in three-piece suits. He wore rimless spectacles—fashionable then, very unfashionable later, fashionable again in the 21st century. His eyes told you that he was unlikely to be misled.

Early each morning, before he went to the bank, he put on old clothes and rubber boots and drove out to the Blue House farm. It was called that because the house on the property, although tenant-less and paint-less (and now, indeed, house-less), had once been blue. Granddad always took with him a pail containing table scraps (the "slops bucket"). The pigs loved the slops and it made good economic sense: Waste not, want not. (He was not quick to dispose of things. When we cleaned out the garage after his death, we found a bucket with a tag tied to it: "This bucket leaks.")

I wonder how many bank presidents slop the hogs. It might give them a better perspective on the world.

RECITATION

I have memorized the opening paragraphs of *The Sweet Science* and *The Earl of Louisiana,* both by Liebling. I didn't set out to learn them; I had read them so many times that they just stuck.

Having learned them, I sometimes thought it would be nice to have an opportunity to display this accomplishment. The occasion was never right. You would be surprised at how thoroughly a recitation of a mere four or five sentences can disrupt a conversation. It is even difficult to insinuate brief excerpts. I found that "It is through Jack O'Brien, the arbiter elegantiarum Philadelphiae, that I trace my rapport with the historic past through the laying on of hands" was not apropos at most dinner parties. Philadelphia Jack O'Brien won the light-heavyweight championship in 1905 by knocking out Bob Fitzsimmons. And the casual remark, "I wonder if Professor Toynbee is as intimately attuned to his sources," merely seemed peculiar. It is true that I have sometimes characterized an acquaintance's observation as "like Golden Bantam trucked up from Texas, stale and unprofitable," but even this is a reach. It does not go down well.

Some of my friends carry with them a supply of well-polished anecdotes, each buffed to a high gloss so that it will slide into talk effortlessly, a verbal ball bearing. This cannot be accomplished with recitation. The success of an inserted anecdote depends on the maintenance of the fiction that it is spontaneous. But, even when the fiction is obvious, an anecdote may be granted a willing suspension of resentment. Recitation, however, will receive no such indulgence.

633 E. MAIN

For the first 95 years of my mother's life, she lived within an area with a half mile radius, beginning on First South Street, the first street south of Main (there is also a Second South, but no Third, and a First North, but no Second). After she married and before her parents died, she lived three blocks away in a house that was a wedding present from her parents. Then she inherited the Main Street house when they died. My father and mother lived at Main Street for thirty years until he died, and she lived in its ten rooms alone for almost another thirty years. From the windows of the second story you can see the house where she was born, on the other side of the block.

The Main Street house is in an area that the local real estate agents refer to, rather wishfully, as "Millionaires Row." It is a frame Victorian, light gray with white trim, three stories tall, with a tower on a front corner — not the most imposing house on the street, but substantial. In my youth, you still saw the original, painted clapboard. In the 1970s, my parents had it covered with vinyl siding. They didn't like paying painters, and they claimed that the ban on lead resulted in paint that wouldn't stick. Decorative architectural details were removed when the siding was put on, and the exterior is now rather plain. Inside, the rooms are handsome, well-proportioned. In the main rooms of the first floor, the doors are nine feet tall and the ceiling height is twelve feet. The quarter sawn oak woodwork has not been painted or altered. The front door, alone, probably has enough oak to make a modern bedroom suite.

A large porch runs along the east side of the house with screens on three sides from floor to ceiling, all twelve feet. If there is any breeze on a summer day, the porch is the place to be. The screen door at the front, which is a little warped, appears to be the original. When my grandparents lived in the house, there was an old wooden swing on the porch, suspended from the ceiling by heavy chains, but the swing was an impediment to foot traffic and my parents disposed of it.

In the front yard, two elderly maples were replaced by sweetgums, which are now large. The sweetgums are handsome and provide shade, but they litter the yard with seed pods about the size of golf balls. As my mother aged and her eyesight faded and she became less steady on her feet, she often stumbled on the fruit and threatened to have the trees removed. They are still there.

In the entry hall, just inside the front door, there is

a large needlepoint portrait of St. Patrick driving the snakes out of Ireland. Snakes curl around the saint's feet and legs. Since this is visible from the front door, it serves to discourage visitors who might otherwise have lingered. There once was a smaller version of the same picture, also in needlepoint, hung in the same place, but that went to my mother's brother when furnishings of the house were distributed after my grandmother's death. A few years later, I saw the large one in an antiques shop in Alton. Local nuns had done needlepoint to raise funds for their Order. Apparently, the pictures came in various sizes. The big one was soiled and the frame was broken, but I had it cleaned and the frame restored. My mother grew up with the image and had a sentimental attachment to it.

In the front parlor, there's an elaborate, large, rococo secretary adorned with carved vines and surmounted by a pediment featuring the head of an exotic young woman, perhaps an Indian maiden descended from an Egyptian priestess. This was acquired when my mother, then a child, went to St. Louis to have her tonsils removed and consequently needed comforting. On the face of it, a 600-pound secretary seems an odd gift for a small girl in the hospital—one might have thought that some nasturtiums would have served—but history must respect the facts. It is also true, however, that the piece was purchased at about the time that my grandparents moved into the Main Street house, and they may have felt the need of furniture that would not be dwarfed by the ceiling height.

The furnishings were a comfortable, highly personal accumulation of the belongings of several branches of the family, reflecting their changing tastes and interests. Twentieth century fashion intruded on the floors and at the windows, but not in its more advanced manifestations. My father was part-owner of a furniture store and had ready access to new carpet, chairs, tables, and sofas. Some were brought home, but the things my parents selected were in a style defined only as mainstream traditional.

When they redecorated the house in the late 1950s, they installed wall-to-wall carpet, covering the hardwood flooring, and they also covered the cut glass fan lights over the windows, substituting upholstered panels and heavy drapes that hid the glass. The first of these innovations lightened the interior a bit; the second did not. The new carpet, beige, manufactured from a man-made fiber with practical cleaning attributes, flowed over the entire expanse of the first floor. The light gained by the reflective power of the carpet was cancelled by the covering of the windows. What the 1950s might grant, it might also take away. My parents had no interest in living in a family museum, and neither did they care about the approval of modernist designers. If they valued the opinion of others, the relevant audience did not extend much beyond Macoupin County.

The parlor is off the main hallway, through a wide opening with heavy, solid oak doors that roll on a track as they disappear into the walls. (I see real estate ads in which some such are called "pocket doors," but the Main Street versions are about the size of pocket battleships.) There is another set of these double doors dividing the parlor from the living room. When my parents installed the wall-to-wall carpet, they pushed the doors back into the walls and left them there. The doors were hidden for more than fifty years.

In my grandparents' time, those doors were closed on special occasions or when serious business was discussed. My grandfather was no longer practicing medicine by the time I was born, but people came to the house to seek his advice on personal matters and community issues, and the parlor served as his office. Sometimes these consultations were confidential.

I recall one occasion when a law enforcement officer arrived during dinner. My grandfather rose from the table, conspicuously draped a large linen napkin over his shoulder, as he always did when the doorbell rang during a meal, and went to the door. Those who came to call seldom failed to get the point: "Oh, Doctor Denby, were you at dinner? I could come back another time." Answer: "Yes, well, my family can eat without me. What can I do for you?" Those visits were usually expeditious. The officer of the law, however, was escorted into the parlor and the doors were closed. I was then about ten, and curious. The story, as I heard it the next day, went like this: My grandparents owned a farm that was rented to brothers who were bachelors. They were good farmers, but they drank, enthusiastically and often. When they came to town, it was an occasion for celebration. On this particular occasion, as on others, the celebration had been excessive, and they were forcibly detained in the drunk tank, locally known as "the calaboose," a facility that was less commodious than the county jail. The officer came to see whether my grandfather would be interested in bailing them out. The farm animals, after all, needed tending, and the bail was less than the price of a cow. Perhaps equally important, the officer asked that my grandfather use his considerable powers of persuasion to guide the brothers onto the straight and narrow path, a task in which both the law and my grandfather eventually proved wanting.

CHURCH

An essay in the 1879 history of the county begins, "The Episcopal church in Macoupin county is small and weak." It still is, but it hangs on. It occupies a handsome, small, frame church built in the mid-19th century using a design taken from Upjohn's pattern book *(Upjohn's Rural Architecture: Designs, Working Drawings and Specifications For a Wooden Church and Other Rural Structures,* 1852). My mother was an Episcopalian and my father was a Lutheran. They were married during one of the several intervals when there were not enough Episcopalians to support a rector, so the wedding took place at home with the Lutheran minister officiating. By the 1940s I was a regular customer of the Episcopal Sunday school, and the only one. Somewhere in the attic of the Main Street house is a perfect attendance badge with hanging appendages for additional years. The Sunday school teacher asked my parents to let her know if there might be a time when I would not be coming—she would welcome the day off. Eventually, the teacher and I both felt that we had exhausted the possibilities for coloring pictures of shepherds and flocks and the like, so we closed down the operation and I became a temporary Presbyterian.

One of my first Sundays with the Presbyterians fell on the day after Christmas, and I arrived dressed in my best clothes. The Sunday school teacher said: "Well, I see you wore all your Christmas presents." That was true; I even had on new shoes. Because I was a newcomer, or perhaps because I was so well-dressed, I was given the honor of carrying the collection plate from the back of the church to deliver it to the minister. The seating sloped down, and there was a metal heating grate in the center of the aisle about halfway down. When my new shoes with leather soles reached the heating grate, my feet went up in the air and so did the plate and all of the coins in it. Most of the collection fell through the grate. There was a gasp from the Presbyterians. Some may have suspected an Episcopal plot to weaken a competitor, but the Presbyterians who knew me attributed it to clumsiness.

A few years later, the Presbyterians and the northern ("American") Baptists, each despairing of continuing to go it alone, joined to form a congregation known as the "Federated." The old Presbyterian church was then torn down and a bank was built on the site. The money changers chased out the temple. I wondered whether the collection was found in the heating duct when the church was demolished.

As is the case elsewhere, old-line Protestant denominations struggle and evangelicals flourish. The Southern Baptists outgrew their modern building, which was only a few years old, and then acquired a very large structure, complete with a commodious parking lot, a place built by Walmart when it first came to town. (Walmart burgeoned even more than the evangelicals. It later built a Super Walmart on a different edge of town.) The church's move into the store caused a political furor and a brief legal hassle because the site was zoned for commercial use and the church took it off the tax rolls.

Carlinville Catholics are now down to one church. Formerly, there were two — St. Mary's, which served those of Irish descent, and St. Joseph's, for the German population. Italians, Poles and Croatians were not consequential when the parishes were established. More recently, dwindling congregations made it impractical to maintain both churches, so a few years ago they merged into a new parish diplomatically named Saints Mary and Joseph. It is located in a new building on the edge of town in a former pasture, neutral turf. The parish house of the former St. Joseph's became Magnolias, a restaurant where ladies lunch. It is probably significant that the Southern Baptists were able to take over a big box store while the German Catholics lost their home to a salad and quiche place.

House With Water View, Adirondacks

FLATWATER CANOEING

Essays about canoeing typically begin with poetic evocation of solitude on a quiet lake. That is sometimes an accurate picture, but canoeing is often noisy, which is not necessarily a bad thing. Canoes are used for fun, and noise is often a part of that.

Noise is not inherent in canoeing. It usually happens because the people are young, have a fine disregard for technique, and are fueled by exuberance or, perhaps, beer. Since canoes are easy to tip and paddles can be used to splash your neighbor, they provide obvious opportunities for rowdiness. There is, nonetheless, something unnatural about noisy canoeing. As the nature writers want to suggest, noise violates a canoe's essential character — or, at least, the character of traditional, wooden canoes.

Wooden canoes are a product of craftsmanship, like a fine piece of furniture. Some are works of art. A century ago, the fanciest were called "courting canoes," and they were used for that purpose. They sometimes came equipped with built-in picnic hampers and hand-cranked phonographs. Modern equipment has changed the sport. Instead of being made of wood and canvas, most canoes are now built with fiberglass, Kevlar, carbon fiber, Royalex, or other plastics. In the decades following World War II, plants that had produced airplanes began making aluminum canoes. These are so durable that many of them are still around. Paddles, formerly wood, are also now made from metal and petrochemicals.

Wood and canvas canoes, when struck, don't resonate. If you hit a wooden canoe with a wooden paddle, you get a modest "thunk." An aluminum canoe, however, hit with a plastic paddle, or almost any paddle, sounds like an ill-tuned calypso drum. A flotilla of them proceeding across a pond is like an audition for a junior high production of *The Harry Belafonte Story*. Loons don't like it.

In its archaic state, flatwater canoeing sometimes approximates the poetic ideal. On flatwater, a canoe glides. If you are skilled and not in a big hurry, you can move silently. It isn't an athletic achievement, but it can be an aesthetic one. "Flatwater" means lakes, ponds, or gentle rivers. Running rapids on fast, rocky rivers is an equally valid art form, but it is not peaceful and not quiet. It requires a different set of skills and is not an activity for a beer party—or, at least, it had better not be. But that is a lecture for another day.

Where I live, there is a lot of water. Canoes were once the principal way that people got around. Horses had limited utility because you couldn't transport them in canoes, and you needed a way to cross lakes. Rivers were welcome, especially for going downstream—with more work, you could also go upstream, either by paddling against the current or by sticking a pole down onto the riverbed and pushing the canoe. A flat-bottom rowboat works better for poling, but it is too heavy to carry across the land between the lakes and rivers. In the Adirondacks, "portage" is put into plain English; it is called a carry. On the other side of the Stony Creek Ponds, across the water from our dock, there is a well-established and popular path known as "The Indian Carry". It was used by the Algonquins to transport furs to the Hudson's Bay Company on the St. Lawrence.

THE PLIMPTON DIVERSION

"Jack Heinz, please."

"Speaking."

"This is George Plimpton."

Oh sure. My first reaction was that it was my friend, Alfred Appel, master of as many as three voices, but all of Alfred's voices were pop singers of an earlier day.

It was, in fact, Plimpton. There was no mistaking the accent—mostly Old Harvard, modified by Paris and Manhattan. He was working on a book about boxing, and an editor at *Sports Illustrated* had suggested that he call me. The book was to include an account of his exhibition bout with Archie Moore, the great Light Heavyweight champion (Moore bloodied Plimpton's nose, and that was the end of it), and he was looking for material about other amateurs who had fought professionals.

I didn't know much, and I told him so. I mentioned Paul Gallico, a sportswriter of the 1920s who got into the ring with Jack Dempsey and was promptly knocked out. Plimpton already knew about that precedent, but hoped the cases might be distinguishable. I then told George (we quickly moved to first names) that in the Regency period, 1811-1820, British aristocrats made boxing a popular form of exercise. Noted pugilists of the day gave lessons to the nobs, providing numerous examples of titled amateurs who sparred with pros. Lord Byron took boxing lessons from John Jackson, the English (and, therefore, world) champion of the 1790s. At that time, boxing was not widely practiced elsewhere. Jackson, I noted, also instructed the Prince Regent and led an honor guard of champions when the Prince became George IV. Warming to the lecture, I mentioned that Byron had a folding screen on which he created a collage of portraits of noted boxers of the 18th and early 19th centuries, in fighting attitude, and that the Prince had in his chambers one of the earliest prints of a match in progress. George had dealt with professors: He was enthusiastic about the illustrative possibilities, thus encouraging me to invest in his project. This was unnecessary. I was already hooked. Since I knew that I had in my library two biographies of British aristocrats who claimed to have boxed with professionals, I said that I would do some research and call him back.

One of the books was an account of the life of Hugh Lowther, the 5th Earl Lonsdale, 1857-1944. He claimed to have knocked out John L. Sullivan when both of them were in their prime. The match took place in great secrecy, of course. Two witnesses supported Lonsdale's version, but they were both members of his faction. I have seen photographs of Lonsdale and he was, in fact, a formidable physical specimen, large, athletic, and fit, and there is no doubt at all that he had a record of impressive accomplishment in the bedroom.

The other book was an account of the exploits of the Queensberrys. The famous Queensberry rules governing boxing were composed with the blessing of the ninth marquess, the one who's son was Oscar Wilde's lover. One of the earlier Queensberrys, known as "Old Q," claimed to have sparred with John Jackson in an exhibition at a dinner party honoring the Tsar of Russia. Old Q, then elderly, arranged for the servants to spill gravy on the floor under Jackson's feet, and the champion slipped and fell. Oh, what good fun! Dinner parties just aren't what they used to be. I called George a day or two later and passed along this material, all of which eventually appeared in his book, *Shadow Box*. George said he felt that he had been given "treasure," and that Norman (Mailer) would be envious. He invited me to come to New York to discuss the book and the history of boxing. I doubt that this was strictly necessary; the trip was probably intended as a reward for my services. But I went.

When *Shadow Box* appeared, it identified me as "John Heinz, a professor of law at Chicago University whose great love is the history of boxing..." My colleagues at Northwestern were delighted by this, but it caused some consternation at the University of Chicago. Moreover, the history of boxing is not, and never was, my great love. Apart from my wife, I have had serious liaisons with modern art, jazz, photography, and any number of writers, living and dead. I courted all of them with far greater ardor than I devoted to boxing. Indeed, from time to time I even generated enthusiasm for that famously jealous mistress, the law.

George graciously invited me to stay at his apartment, which was decorated with posters by Andy Warhol, Larry Rivers, Willem de Kooning, and Helen Frankenthaler, all of them designed as fund-raisers for *The Paris Review*. There is a good description of the apartment in George's novel, *The Curious Case of Sidd Finch*. Finch is a baseball pitcher and Buddhist monk whose fastball exceeds 160 mph, owing to Karma. His apartment closely resembles Plimpton's.

The other members of the Plimpton family were in the Hamptons. George and I talked boxing for an hour or so. I mentioned that in the bare knuckle days it was common for a fighter's backers to dose him with laudanum (i.e., opium) to dull the pain, and George commented that this seemed likely to slow him down. True enough, I said, but bare knuckle fights were not about speed or footwork—the objective was to remain standing, having absorbed great punishment.

After a bit of this, George departed for a business meeting and we agreed to meet at the Racquet Club on Park Avenue at 5:30. I showed up at the appointed hour and told the doorman that George Plimpton had asked me to meet him there. I was welcomed graciously, and invited to make myself at home. Mr. Plimpton would be informed that I was waiting. Since no particular waiting area was designated, I strolled about the place. It is an ersatz Italian Renaissance palazzo, adorned with paintings and prints of upper crust sports—polo, fox hunting, archaic forms of tennis. The club houses a court for "real" tennis, a facsimile of the game played by Henry VIII at Hampton Court. Larger than a lawn tennis court and enclosed on all sides, it has sloping roofs known to the cognoscenti as "penthouses," openings or windows into which balls may be hit, and a buttress off of which shots are played. The balls are made of cork, wrapped in cloth, and are heavier than lawn tennis balls, less bouncy. The court is asymmetric. All of this allegedly reproduces some building in medieval France. Needless to say, very few of these courts exist in the U.S., a circumstance that both reflects and preserves the social exclusivity of the game. George was an accomplished player of real or "court" tennis; in 1961, he was the runner-up for the club championship. A brief history of the club, privately printed in the early 1960s, comments: "George is a great one for going into various games and he has made considerable progress at both court tennis and racquets."

Sometime after six, I tired of looking at 19th century sporting prints and George had not arrived, so I repaired to the bar and had a scotch with a bit of water while watching the denizens play cribbage. Of course, as in most such places, it was not possible to pay for the drink with actual money. Instead, I was given something to sign, obviously intended for members. I was apprehensive that more than a decade in teaching might have so eroded my appearance and manner that I would be tossed out of the joint, but I confidently signed the chit "George Plimpton" and nobody gave a damn. I think it was John O'Hara who said that a man in a seersucker suit can cash a check anywhere.

The scotch being gone and George not having appeared, I went looking for him. I found my way to the library, and there, at the other end of a large, open room, I saw George seated on a chesterfield, engaged in quiet conversation with another man. I hailed him from across the room — and was promptly shushed by George and others. My enthusiasm at finding him had carried me away, but I'm quite certain that I did not disturb any scholarly work.

George suggested dinner at Elaine's, another of

his regular haunts. The restaurant was then in only its second decade (now it is in its fifth), but it was already known as a gathering place for writers and entertainers, including Mailer, Gay Talese, Woody Allen, David Halberstam, and the *Saturday Night Live* crowd. We did not see any of them. The restaurant is considerably less showy than its customers—indeed, it is a modest, unassuming, checkered tablecloth place. We joined a table at which three or four other men, all of them George's acquaintances, were already seated. I was introduced around. If I had a better memory or was more familiar with the New York literary establishment, I might be able to identify our companions. I do remember that George ordered only spaghetti with butter, which impressed me. I don't know whether that was his regular fare.

George asked the group to attribute the saying, "He was not born in the woods to be scared by an owl," which he wanted to use as the epigraph of *Shadow Box*. This was clearly intended as a reference to Muhammad Ali, who figures prominently in the book, but I don't think that George had any particular owl in mind. We were all stumped, but George was not deterred. The epigraph appears in the book, unattributed. (Now, with the aid of the internet, we can find it in a story by Harriet Spofford, "Circumstance," published in *The Atlantic* in 1860.)

Early the next morning, George left to join his

family in the Hamptons for the weekend. I woke in time to see him picked up by Jerzey Kosinski. My wife was arriving from Chicago, and George invited the two of us to stay on in the apartment. It would have been pleasant to stay there, but I felt uncomfortable about making ourselves at home after only a brief acquaintance, so we went to the St. Regis instead, which was then under Sheraton management and considerably less expensive than it later became. I told George that the St. Regis had romantic associations. This was not strictly true, but it was the sort of reason that George favored.

Shortly after the book was published, George invited me to one of his parties, which were legendary. I was, however, passing through a serious scholar phase, and I decided to stay in Chicago and work. It was a poor decision. His parties were well-lubricated gatherings of literary New York. Jonathan Dee, a novelist who was once an editorial assistant at *The Paris Review,* said that George "would always order 38 bottles of Scotch, one bottle of white wine and a bottle of Dubonnet, and it was always a struggle to get him to order food." *People* magazine covered George's 50th birthday party in March of 1977 and published a four-page photo spread showing, among the guests, Jacqueline Kennedy Onassis, Woody Allen, Lauren Bacall, and an actress who emerged from a cake wearing a gorilla suit—and who a few minutes later wore nothing at all. *People* said, "Though George Plimpton's rep is as a jack-of-all-trades, he is unquestionably master of one: throwing a party."

I missed the party, but I did see George two or three times during my visits to New York in the late 1970s. On one of those occasions, he showed me a large stack of 8 x 10 prints of shots that *People* had not used. George smiled broadly as we looked through the pictures. He loved parties.

In September, Muhammad Ali fought Ernie Shavers, a hard puncher, and George suggested that I join him at ringside, but tickets were scarce and I was parsimonious. George sent me a letter with his reactions, mostly about the locker rooms after the fight. He closed the letter, "Do keep in touch." But I didn't. I should have

Patriotic Bear, Vermont

DROSTEN'S

Drosten's restaurant had a long table at the rear reserved for lawyers. The courthouse was only three blocks away, and lawyers from other towns often joined the locals for conversations that were spirited and almost always audible. There was a pressed tin ceiling, figured wallpaper, worn wood floors, ceiling fans, old oak tables, equally old chairs, and a mahogany back-bar salvaged from some saloon, but no alcohol. It was the sort of restaurant where you could get baked chicken with dressing. Just inside the front door, near the cash register, there was a long, low ice cream cooler, the kind that resembles an oversized coffin. You could have ice cream for dessert, if you were somewhat lacking in imagination, or you could stop for a cone on your way home from school, but not many kids did because Drosten's was a serious place. In the kitchen, ladies who lived on farms did much of the cooking. They enhanced not only their family income but the quality of Carlinville life. The pie crusts were made with real lard. The plum pies were reason enough to live there.

Otis O'Neill owned a hardware store west of the

Marvel Theater. He was a bachelor, and a regular at Drosten's, where he always ordered a bowl of soup. (Good choice! The vegetable soup was excellent.) As he ate, he leaned farther and farther over the bowl, just in case the napkin tucked into his collar was insufficient to preserve the shirt for another day. Mr. O'Neill had a broad skull that supported hair only at its nether reaches, so his combover had to cover a lot of territory. The left plot, mostly uncut, was assigned the task of bridging the full expanse, all the way to where hair began again on the right. At a neighboring table, we entertained ourselves betting on how long it would be before the stress produced by the lean over the soup overcame the adhesive power of Wildroot Cream Oil. No money was placed on periods beyond three minutes. We doubted that the Wildroot improved the soup.

Another frequent diner at Drosten's was Harold Wentworth, a professor at Blackburn College and co-author of the *Dictionary of American Slang*. One evening when Professor Wentworth was there, my mother leaned over to me and whispered, "That book has naughty words in it." She was joking. More precisely, she was mimicking the critique heard in local literary circles.

Social mores made it difficult to get through a meal at Drosten's. The townspeople regarded it as impolite to enter or leave without stopping by the tables of their friends to chat or pay their respects and, in a small town, there are many friends. This required the gentlemen at the visited table, from about the age of six, to stand to receive the guests — and to remain standing throughout the visit while the pork chop congealed on the plate. One was not permitted to slip a small piece of a roll into the mouth while standing. Many of the ladies who visited our table said "Please don't stand," but they did not have the power to release me from the dictates of propriety. This was a test of character. Self-denial is a lesson to be learned early.

I'm told that before I reached standing-up age, while I was still in a highchair, I tended to throw chicken legs, limbering-up my pitching arm. The problem was solved by tying a string around the chicken leg and tying the other end of it around the arm of the highchair. This restricted my range, but did little to promote decorum. The string prevented the chicken leg from reaching other diners, but it was long enough to permit me to pitch it.

A PROPER BREAKFAST

There are those who feel that a real breakfast is bacon and eggs. I am, indeed, very fond of the traditional English breakfast—that is, eggs, preferably up, streaky bacon, a sausage with a high bread content, grilled tomato, and unbuttered toast served upright in a silver rack where it has reposed for a decent interval, the slices having been separated to permit the circulation of air. Toast of that kind has structural integrity. But I regard that meal as lunch or even a dinner.

My standard breakfast, and my preferred breakfast if I can't get oatmeal, is shredded wheat. Not the little bite size version, but the original biscuits—each of which is about the size of a *pain au chocolat,* but much more satisfactory. In their manufactured state, however, the sharp corners of the original biscuits do not rest comfortably in a curved bowl. They should be crushed. They come packaged in sets of three, wrapped in real paper, not polypropylene. (They did when I wrote this.) This presents a problem. If removed from the packaging and then crushed, the biscuits tend to shatter. Fragments scatter across the table. This is untidy.

One, then, has a series of choices. If you crush all three biscuits before opening the paper wrapper, you may feel obliged to consume them all. But three is too sumptuous a serving, so you may wish to share. But dividing them into portions once crushed is imprecise, likely to lead to quarrels, and the paper wrapper may well have been damaged by the crushing process, exposing the remaining portion to humidity and weevils. Yet, a single biscuit is clearly not enough for a man of my size.

The obvious solution is to locate a mate who can make do with only one biscuit, This may seem an odd reason for selecting a mate, but it is at least as sensible as the more usual criteria. Once you have found the right partner, you must then devise a method for isolating the one biscuit and crushing it without dispersion while retaining the other two within the wrapper where they can be disassembled efficiently and hygienically. There are two possible approaches. The first is to delegate this problem to your mate. This is entirely satisfactory, so long as you can get away with it. The other is referred to as the "partial crush." In this procedure, one of the three biscuits—preferably one located near an end of the package, not the biscuit in the middle—is damaged but not destroyed. Its sharp corners are rounded off, as it were, the package is then opened, and one biscuit is extracted, including its shards. This requires some technique. The paper package is then re-closed by folding the paper, and the remaining two are crushed while confined. This needs to be done carefully in order to avoid tearing the paper. As you can see, this is a bit more complicated and can easily go wrong.

Anne and I are perfectly compatible. I eat two biscuits and she eats one, even though she refers to it as "straw." Strains occur in any marriage, of course. Should Anne be away or, God forbid, decline to eat her biscuit, I am "left in a logical cleft stick from which I have but one escape." Disposing of a perfectly good biscuit is unacceptable. How, then, to crush two and leave one biscuit still in the package, more or less intact? I have found that this is best addressed by an extension—a redoubling, as it were—of the partial crush. Should Anne be away for two days, I in due course crush both of the remaining biscuits in their respective wrappers and have a full serving. Her absence for a week or more, however, may call for desperate measures, such as Cheerios.

Shredded wheat is best with milk and wheat germ. Anne refers to wheat germ as "sawdust," and draws the line, but the germ comes in a form that permits easy division. I see no reason why her fancy should not be indulged. The autocrat of the breakfast table now has highly-developed sensitivity.

In my younger days, of course, I would have scoffed at the notion that this is a proper breakfast. I don't hold with those who say that age brings wisdom, balance, and judgment, but there does come a time to put aside childish things. And, for that matter, put aside almost everything else.

ON NOT BEING J. P. DONLEAVY

I have in my office a pristine, hardbound copy of J. P. Donleavy's *A Singular Country* that I bought from the Evanston Public Library for one dollar. It still has the long, white slip where "date due" could be recorded, but the slip is virginal. Apparently the book never left the library's shelves. This surprised me. When I was an undergraduate, Donleavy's *The Ginger Man*, a picaresque novel set in Dublin, had considerable success, aided by the fact that it was declared obscene in both the US and Ireland. The internet tells me it is still in print and has sold 45 million copies.

Donleavy, although New York City born and raised, was a professional Irishman. After serving in the U. S. Navy during WWII, he attended Trinity College, Dublin, for a time, and *The Ginger Man* bought him a two-hundred acre estate in Ireland, complete with eighteenth century manor house.

The jacket of *A Singular Country* quotes *The Guardian*, "This is absolutely wildly funny—and cutting—first rate stuff from the world champ stage Irishman," and from *The New Yorker*, "No contemporary writer is better than Donleavy at his best," and

Joseph Heller, "Donleavy is one of the most accomplished and original writers of our time." Why didn't those blurbs catch the eye and encourage someone, anyone, to borrow the book?

I keep the unread book in my office to remind me of the transience, the flimsiness, of fame. It comforts me when my books don't sell. One could even argue that I'm more fortunate than Donleavy, that it may be better to have avoided fame. If you were once well-known, you know that you were considered, perhaps even debated, and then rejected. You can't think that you were simply overlooked, unseen. This, it strikes me, is akin to the old question of whether it is better to have loved and lost than never to have loved at all. See Tennyson. If you have some real affection for another person, you are, at least, not wholly self-regarding. It suggests that you were willing to venture out into the world. The same observation applies to writing and painting, which are communicative acts. You do them because you have something you want to say, some gesture you want to express. But if your writing isn't read or your painting isn't seen, you haven't communicated.

Perhaps we do the work only to record the fact that we were here, that we passed this way and did something more productive than consuming natural resources. The desire for a record explains why both writings and paintings are ordinarily signed, even though the signature will mean little or nothing to most people.

It does not explain pseudonyms. Presumably, we want credit for good work and we perhaps hope to avoid discredit or censure for bad. But why did Samuel Clemens sign his classics Mark Twain and why did Eric Blair hide behind George Orwell? Often, authors are unsure about how the work will be received. Or perhaps, more generously, the use of a pseudonym is a statement that only the quality of the work counts, not the identity of its creator. John Banville used the name Benjamin Black when he wanted to distinguish his mystery stories from his serious literary work. But then someone told him that he was often better as Black than he was as Banville, and on reflection he agreed with that, so he dropped the pseudonym. The mysteries are now acknowledged Banvilles. Most artists and writers, however, take the risk and seek the credit.

Despite such conspicuous examples as Liberace, it is difficult to set aside the ridiculous but ingrained notion that fame indicates worth. If merit reliably generated fame, everyone would know the name A. J. Liebling. They don't. This can't be attributed to the lack of a record. Liebling had a long and successful career at *The New Yorker* and he wrote marvelous books, especially *The Sweet Science, The Earl of Lousiana*, and *Between Meals: An Appetite for Paris*, books filled with evidence of his wit, his critical judgment, and his zest for life. He is remembered by some (not all) serious writers, of course, people in the business, just as Enos Slaughter and Red Schoendienst are remembered by baseball fans—but that's a narrower sort of fame—fame among scholars.

Any reasonably sane person welcomes praise for good work. Writers and artists, in particular, like evidence that they were able to do something, some well-defined thing, really well. They usually have ambition, at least, for a high level of achievement. There are many prizes in the arts, but often the only real reward is hearing that the work gave pleasure.

I was raised in a small town in the Middle West in a culture where ambition was monitored and rationed. One of the pieces of survival advice I got there was that you should avoid being seen as full of yourself. Ambition, while generally acceptable and perhaps even useful, could easily go wrong. Fame outside the town was especially suspect, not only because the judgment of strangers could not be trusted but because seeking wider fame suggested that the person had an inflated estimate of his ability. (Football players were granted an exception.) High achievers made us uncomfortable. Students who did well in school needed to worry that they would be called the teacher's pet; not a label associated with social success. Envy motivated much of this conduct, of course, but it nonetheless dampened career plans.

J. P. Donleavy died near his home in Ireland in 2017 without having learned that *A Singular Country* sat unread at the Evanston Public Library. He was spared that. I'm sure he worked on the manuscript for many hours and hoped that the book would be read with pleasure.

Just Take a Little Off the Top, Pennsylvania

INTERVIEWED BY THE FBI

One day, while working at the Pentagon, an FBI agent came to see me. The first question he asked was, "Do you play poker?"

"No."

"Never?"

"No."

"Why not?"

What was this about? Was he fishing for poker analogies? Something about bluffing or holding your cards, or standing pat, or some such?

He said, "Why not?" Again.

"Probably because I'm not patient enough, I suppose. I don't like card games, generally. Or board games. Or puzzles."

He was a small man, middle-aged, dressed in a brown suit as I recall it, someone who was likely to blend in. We were in my office, a ten-foot square with a window that had a view of a blank wall of the C ring, a few feet away. At least I wasn't summoned; he came to me.

The agent opened his file and pretended to read it. I knew that he didn't need to and he knew that I knew. He was trying to decide how direct he should be. With a smile, not a warm one, he said, "I've been told that some of the officers who work at the White House have a regular game." Ah, so this is about the White House.

"You don't play?"

"No, I don't."

He opened his file again. More fake reading.

"Do you have any friends among the aides at the White House?"

"Sure. I'm a social aide, as I'm sure your file tells you. I work with all of them and I guess I'm friendly with all of them, more or less."

"Do you know Major John Costello or Lieutenant Colonel James Martin?" [These are pseudonyms.]

"Sure. I work with both of them."

"Do you like them?"

"Yes. They're both good officers from what I can see. Both good men. You understand that we're only social aides. Mostly, we just go to White House parties and stand around in fancy uniforms with lots of braid and look decorative. We're part of the background that tells the guests that they're at the White House."

"You sound cynical."

"An occupational hazard. But I do my job."

"I'm told that you do. Tell me more about Major Costello and Colonel Martin."

What does he want? OK. "Jack Costello's day job is as a legislative liaison for the Army. He's interested in politics, and good at it, and he deals with Congressional staff on constituent inquiries or complaints involving the Army. Colonel Martin is older, of course, works in Air Force contract management—contracts with airframe manufacturers, I think. He was a bomber pilot."

"I notice that you refer to Major Costello as 'Jack' but to Colonel Martin as 'Colonel.' Why?"

"I have a rule of thumb that I go by. Officers who are only one rank above me can be called by their first names; but officers more than one rank above me get their title. It's a matter of courtesy." I could have added that it also keeps me out of trouble.

A short time later, the FBI man left. I'd be interested to see what his report said.

I didn't know during the interview that Walter Jenkins, the White House chief of staff, had been arrested in the men's room of a YMCA near the White House and charged with homosexual conduct. It was October of 1964 and the presidential election campaign was the main show in Washington. Lyndon Johnson was running against Barry Goldwater, and Walter Jenkins was the president's long-time assistant and advisor.

Johnson was far enough ahead of Goldwater to withstand one homosexual in the White House, but the disclosure of more might have been damaging. It was not long after the McCarthy era. There was a quiet hunt going on, and the all-male, all-unmarried social aides were a likely place to look. The investigation identified girlfriends, some of whom were interviewed; social networks were examined. As it turned out, Major Costello and Colonel Martin were both discharged. Apparently, there was some sort of regular poker game, perhaps a cover story. They were both career officers. Two careers ended. Collateral damage.

ON ACADEMIC ACHIEVEMENT

An academic who is given to envy is in for a hard time. The number of people who might be envied is large. It includes both those in other occupations (doctors and lawyers, hedge fund manipulators, media pundits) and one's colleagues. The difference is that, in the academic world, the rewards are mostly symbolic. Who got the endowed chair or won the latest prize? Who got the corner office?

The average academic's world is tiny. A scholar is regarded as famous if as many as two dozen people think that his or her work is significant. We know this—we keep track of such things through compilations of who cites whom, such as the Social Science Citation Index and Google Scholar. Last year a university press published a small piece of 19th century American history. It had Lincoln in the title (a big plus in computer searches). By the end of a year after publication, the book had sold 200 copies. I know; I was the co-author. The book will not continue selling at that rapid pace once the libraries have stopped acquiring it. This is a typical case. Some scholarly books have even smaller sales. In the late 20th century, press runs at university presses were commonly as low as 100 and seldom more than 1000. Now many are printed only "on demand," and there isn't much of that.

Why, then, does anyone choose to become an academic? Few people do, of course, but more would if they could — there are dozens of applications for every university job. Two reasons: 1) There is plenty of new stuff to think about. Boredom is more often the product of sloth than of necessity. 2) The work can be, and sometimes is, exquisitely satisfying. The opportunity to create new knowledge, however trivial, is not given to many, and the nurture of students who appear to gain in insight, some of whom subsequently find productive places in the world, gives the teacher a feeling of accomplishment, sometimes deserved. But the scholar cannot count on basking in glory, whether reflected from students or conferred by colleagues. True scholars set their own standards. This is probably the principal reason why so many fail: they do not set them high enough.

MAJOR BURKE

In the living room of the Main Street house, a portrait of one of my great-great-grandfathers, Beatty T. Burke, hangs over the fireplace. The portrait, which is large and elaborately framed, was produced through a 19th century photographic process and then mounted on linen and enhanced with charcoal and white chalk. It shows a middle-aged man with abundant hair, piercing, dark eyes, a bushy mustache, and a narrow beard in the style known as an imperial, after the one worn by Napoleon III.

Beatty Burke admired the romantic poets, especially Byron, and named his first son Don Alonzo. In the 1830s, Beatty was elected Major of a regiment of Illinois militia, and for the remainder of his life he was styled Major Burke. He served as sheriff of the county for many years, and later was a senator in the state legislature.

While sheriff, he faced down a lynch mob at the county jail. The governor had signed a reprieve for a convicted murderer, which was an unpopular decision. As reported in the *History of Macoupin County* published in 1879:

The next morning an immense crowd gathered from all parts of the county to witness the execution. When they found it would not take place, they threatened vengeance against the murderer, and excited and agitated, they rushed for the jail, and gathered a howling, frenzied mob around the building, determined to take the prisoner out by force and lynch him. One of the murdered man's brothers was in the crowd. But the sheriff was a man of great personal bravery, and standing his ground manfully in defense of law and order, by appeals to the crowd and an exhibition of determined courage, held them at bay.

While the mob was threatening, however, the prisoner, "hearing the cries of those who sought his life," hanged himself in his cell. Major Burke's commission as sheriff, dated August 21, 1838, hangs in the hallway of the Main Street house.

There is also a rather good oil painting of peonies, done by my great-grandmother Burke (the wife of Don A) in the late 19th century, when proper gentlewomen either painted or played the piano. Her name was Tennessee and, by all accounts, she was a formidable character. She lived to be nearly 100 years old, at a time when that age was much more rare than it is today. At the age of 97, believing that a basket she wanted might have been left in the hayloft of the barn, she climbed a ladder to the loft and looked for it. She was eager to assert her vigor. At a community meeting held when Tennie was in her mid-nineties, a prize was given to the oldest person in attendance; a woman in her eighties claimed the prize and Tennie deferred to the woman's seniority.

Tennie's daughter, my maternal grandmother, was a free spirit. She was sent to a school in St. Louis for young ladies and was taught to play the piano, quite well. Her house always had a piano, but I never heard her play. In my day, her hands were arthritic. She was short and plump, bright and witty, Irish and proud of it. In public, she was proper, but at home she was full of fun and had a taste for mischief. In her late sixties, she would skip around the house chanting:

> Rooty tee toot
> rooty tee toot
> we are the girls from the Institute.
> We don't smoke
> and we don't chew
> and we don't go
> with the boys who do.
> Our class won the bible!

Her obituary in the local newspaper was accompanied by a photo of her sitting in the parlor next to a melodeon. Sedately. Her grandchildren loved her.

My father's side of the family does not have a large presence in the house. There is, however, hanging next to Major Burke's commission as sheriff, a certificate attesting to the election of Peter Heinz, my great-grandfather, as mayor of Carlinville. Peter arrived from Germany via New Orleans in 1853, and he became mayor in 1876. An American story. According to the 1879 *History of Macoupin County:*

> *In 1848 he became involved with Schurz, Hecker and other German patriots, in the insurrection and revolution, which had for its object the overthrow of the then existing tyrannical form of government, and the establishment of a republic. The attempt, as is well known, was unsuccessful. He was arrested and placed in prison, where he remained fourteen days. As soon as he received his liberty he determined to quit the country.*

The fact that he was incarcerated for only fourteen days suggests that he was not a major player in the revolution.

Peter was a cabinetmaker, and the Main Street house holds a small chair that is his work.

THE ITS

When I entered Washington University in the fall of 1954, the trains of the Illinois Terminal System still ran from downtown Carlinville to downtown St. Louis near the riverfront. The trains ran on electricity, cross-country, through farmers' fields, in effect an assembly of streetcars coupled together. In the mid 1950s, the trains were still heated by cast-iron pot-bellied stoves and the seats were caned. The line didn't last much longer. The tracks were pulled up decades ago.

From the ITS terminal in St. Louis, I took the "University" streetcar line out Olive Street, past Grand Avenue, through the Central West End, then past Forest Park, with the art museum and the zoo, to Washington U. Along the way, we went by Boyle and Olive, a neighborhood then crowded with antiques shops. Less than a decade later it became known as Gaslight Square, the nightlife district. A restaurant called Smokey Joe's Grecian Terrace did business there, persisting through both the antiques era and the pricey saloons. Joe Cunningham, a St. Louis Cardinals outfielder, lived upstairs over the restaurant, so his teammates called him Smokey Joe Cunningham. He was noted for entertaining young women at his digs, with enthusiasm. A tornado hit Gaslight Square during the night in 1959 and did some damage to the restaurant. A TV station asked Cunningham what he had been doing when the tornado hit. He replied, "Reading my Bible."

Tree as Manet's Olympia

CLOTHES MAKE THE MAN

When I was in high school, maybe a junior or a senior, I worked at a YMCA camp in northern Wisconsin. I was a waterfront instructor—swimming, boats, waterskiing. I had a good tan. I got the job because one of my high school teachers was the camp director. The Y, however, was located in Chicago and all of the other counselors were from the city. This meant that I was culturally distinct. My accent was somewhat different and I didn't know good salami from dreck. The most obvious difference, however, was that I wore boxer-style swimming trunks and they all wore Speedo-type racing suits, skintight. My trunks were standard issue for the ponds near Carlinville, as their suits were for the pools in Chicago.

This difference brought unanticipated social consequences. It was a boy's camp, but the kitchen and dining room were staffed by girls from nearby small towns, mostly Hayward. In their off hours, the girls lounged at the waterfront, and they were understandably observant. They attended closely to the Speedos, and they noted that my trunks were considerably more voluminous, which apparently led to speculation. After dinner one night, one of the girls worked up her courage just far enough to ask me why I didn't wear a little suit like the other boys. I declined to answer, which of course served to stimulate the speculation. I was not about to spoil the illusion.

THE CHILI PARLOR

In the first edition of *Roadfood*, by Jane and Michael Stern, the maps show Carlinville. This is noteworthy because maps in that book are supposed to include only towns with recommended restaurants or with enough size to make them useful for navigation. But no Carlinville café is noted in the book. A puzzle.

I have, however, constructed a theory about why Carlinville appears in the *Roadfood* maps. Essentially, it comes down to this: the excellence of the local cuisine could not be ignored. But Carlinville is 12 miles from Interstate 55, far from the path beaten by the madding crowd that the publisher's marketing department hoped to reach.

The Sterns knew about Carlinville, I think. They are persons of sophistication, a woman and man of the world. No doubt they had heard about Carlinville's food, or perhaps even consumed it. They may have been thinking of Roper's Dairy Bar, but the more likely candidates are Drosten's or Taylor's Chili Parlor. When *Roadfood* was first published, in 1977, the owners of Drosten's had not yet retired, and the restaurant was still performing at the standard of excellence it achieved throughout its long life. As I have noted elsewhere, it was a classic of the baked chicken and pressed tin ceiling variety, Otis O'Neill's favorite dining establishment, the place where chicken legs were tied to my highchair to limit their range. Oh, what I would give today for some of that vegetable soup or plum pie!

But Taylor's is perhaps the more likely possibility. A canned version of its chili was sold throughout Macoupin County. The legend is that Charles O. Taylor, who made no claim to Mexican ancestry, received the recipe from a man he bailed out of jail in St. Louis in 1904, when Taylor went there for the World's Fair. In one version of the story, the chili formula was bargained for—it was exchanged for the bail money—and, in another, it was a reward for Mr. Taylor's generosity, thus reinforcing the faith that a benefaction is returned a thousand-fold. In yet another account of the Creation, one that is somewhat less cinematic, Taylor worked at the Mexican pavilion at the World's Fair and thus acquired the art.

In my lifetime, the Chili Parlor has moved several times, but always within Carlinville. In my youth and for several years thereafter, it occupied a building along the interurban railroad tracks, a block from the square. The canning operation, now under separate management from the Parlor, is still in that location. The restaurant then moved one block away, to the dining room of the old Heinz Hotel on West Main Street, and later, in what I think of as a lapse of judgment, it moved to the party room of The Glades, a restaurant on the outskirts of town. But the Chili Parlor is now in a building that formerly housed the Anchor Inn, a saloon also known as Sheik and Jerk's (for its owners, Sheik Fornero and Jerk Selvo), in an alley off the square. The barroom remains, connected to the restaurant, and locals still call it the Anchor.

The first location was manned by generations of Taylors, always with a firm hand. It served only chili, butterbean soup, and vegetable soup, with unsalted crackers. Nothing else; no nonsense. To drink, you could have water or two kinds of soda—orange or cream, as I recall it. No colas, no coffee or tea, and certainly no alcohol. You would take what they gave you, and like it. And we did. The bowls came in two sizes, small and large. You could order a large chili, perhaps supplemented by a small butterbean. As you can see, this provided a considerable range of options.

The old place along the interurban tracks had a counter and half a dozen tables. The tables were solid oak, thick, and were scrubbed every day with bleach, so that they were nearly white. The floor was covered with sawdust. You did not rearrange the tables to accommodate a group. The Taylors would descend upon you.

The chili is spicy. Back when tapioca was regarded

as a taste treat, Taylor's was a challenge. But in this age of excess, when the competition serves up a bowl of red pepper, the chili seems merely flavorful. Its more distinctive characteristic is the fat content. You see it in the bowl, floating on top. If it were not for the elderly people at adjoining tables who have eaten the stuff for years, you might be inclined to worry.

My paternal grandfather, referring to my other grandfather, was fond of saying as he approached his large chili, "Doc Denby won't eat this stuff." When my father was young, the family lived in a house next door to the Chili Parlor. The Heinz backyard adjoined the Parlor's side yard. My grandfather would send my father out the back door with a quart dinner pail and instruct him to bring it back filled with chili. The Taylors and the Heinzes had a relationship that the writers for the quarterlies would call symbiotic. Because the meat that went into the chili was not government inspected (in those days), it could not be shipped in interstate commerce, but the chili (then, as now) had fans far and wide. So the Parlor would receive orders for cases of canned chili from hungry customers in Lompoc or Schenectady. Mr. Taylor would then bring the case over to the Heinz Furniture Store, a half block away, to wrap the package in paper that prominently said "Heinz Furniture." We never knew what he did with those packages, of course.

The Taylors are Catholics. Chili was available on Fridays, for purchase by heathens or apostates, but the Taylors thoughtfully provided for their coreligionists. Butterbean was the Friday soup. The label on the butterbean cans said, "There Is No Meat Or Meat Product In This Soup." But the butterbean is not for the fainthearted. Black pepper replaces the red, and there is plenty of it. (You can see it in the soup.) And, although it is meatless, it is not fatless. All the recipes are secret, but we know about the fat because, although the butterbean is no longer canned, it is available in a box, dry, in a build-it-yourself kit. The assembly instructions say: "You will need 1 stick butter." (The stick is a unit of measure equal to one-quarter pound.) The box includes only dried beans for you to soak, and spices. I don't know why the soup is no longer canned—it seemed to be reasonably stable; the flavor was good. But it is still served in the Parlor, and some customers prefer it to the chili. The color is rich, not red like the chili, of course, but a strong orange, somewhere between pumpkin and burnt sienna.

The third soup, vegetable, was quite bland but very good. It was the sensible option for the member of your family with ulcers, heartburn, or severe gastric distress. The vegetable soup wasn't canned, and it is no longer served in the Parlor. The vegetables in the soup were very finely chopped. In the days before food processors, this required considerable handwork. The recipe was secret, of course, but it was clear that the predominant ingredient was cabbage. Some said that this explained why it was never canned. The cans would explode.

The Chili Parlor may be too far from the interstate to qualify for inclusion in *Roadfood*, but it is now accessible in cyberspace. At www.taylorschili.com, you can order 6, 12, or 24 can cases of the chili (with government-inspected beef) or the butterbean assembly kits delivered to your own home, and you can view a picture of the historic Parlor as it was for 63 years, from 1919 to 1982. You can enjoy your virtual chili in your own virtual parlor, but Mr. Taylor won't tell you that you can't move your table. Too bad.

Homage to Bernadine Loges, Coreys

WEST MAIN STREET

If you walk Main Street from west to east, you start by Major Burke's mansion, which is set well back from the road, near the city limit. The bricks of the walkway from the road to the house are still there but you don't see them. They were set a foot or more below the lawn, so that there was a raised border or curb of grass on both sides. Over the years, the curb eroded, depositing soil on the bricks, and grass spread over the paving. The walk now looks like the dry bed of a small stream, covered by two or three inches of dirt, the accumulation of a century and a half.

I saw the inside of the house once, more than sixty years ago, when it was still a private residence. I've not been there since. It's now a funeral home that does a brisk trade, and a considerable portion of the lawn has been given over to parking for the bereaved. One of the realities of the funeral business is that friends of the deceased are likely to be elderly and to require parking nearby on smooth pavement.

Walking east toward town you soon come to the old Walmart, now abandoned by the mercantilists and serving as the tabernacle of a fundamentalist evangelical congregation. It stands on the site where a commercial iris field once blossomed. Behind that field was Mr. Opper's strawberry farm where I had my first real pay job, picking. Also in that neighborhood is a home for the elderly called Morse's Farm, a recent addition. It isn't a farm. But I'm told it's nice. Maybe soon. I went to school with some of the Morses. They owned neither the iris field nor the strawberry patch, but they did have a small apple orchard farther from town.

Then you come to the high school. From the exterior, it looks much as it did in my time except that they have added several outbuildings devoted to athletics. There has been a great expansion of parking lots. Our athletic events in the 1950s were less well-housed, and not many students then had cars. I lived in town, but I had a Cushman motorscooter. My chemistry teacher told me I should take it home so that my mother could do the washing. It was a time when washing machines were, or recently had been, powered by small gasoline engines.

Despite the external appearance of the school, the interior is new. The building burned three decades ago and a replacement with a new floor plan was constructed inside the old shell. The scene of my triumphs and humiliations is no more. Just as well, I suppose. Of the two sorts of memories, the humiliations are clearer.

And then you come to the railroad crossing, with a stoplight. The light arrived about a decade ago, and it is one of only two or three in the town. North of the crossing, grain elevators stand next to the tracks, a shipping point that brings farmers to town. South of the crossing, there was a frame station—clapboard painted grey, rather austere but clearly Victorian, a scene from Grant Wood—with a waiting room, bathrooms, and a telegrapher. The telegrapher told you how late the train was going to be. The line was then owned by the Gulf, Mobile & Ohio, which ran trains with club cars and with dining cars that served chess pie. When Amtrak took over, it promptly got rid of the club car, the dining car, and the chess pie. Then they tore down the old station. But trains still stop there, and there is a new building with clean lines, a layer of brick over something-or-other, and poured concrete floors that don't squeak. And the trains are still late.

Immediately on the other side of the tracks are two important sites. The more prominent is Boente's Shell station. This venerable dispensary of gasoline and auto repairs is owned by the family of Dana Boente, who briefly served as Acting Attorney General of the United States in early 2017 during one of the Trump Administration's frequent periods of indecision. Across the street from the station, the Boentes formerly had a petroleum "bulk plant"—that is, a place where oil was stored and then distributed. If the soil on that site is not impervious to water, I don't know why not.

Next door to the bulk plant was a restaurant called "The Spot." It was the sort of place known as a family restaurant, offering a choice of a hamburger and a Coke or the blue plate special, but it was noteworthy for its interior décor, which anticipated psychedelia by about two and a half decades. The ceiling was painted with bands of primary colors that extended down the walls and threatened the floors. On one memorable occasion, I took my younger brother and sister, then quite young, to The Spot for dinner. I was babysitting. Christmas was impending and I had taken both of them to the Episcopal church for a rehearsal of the Sunday school Nativity pageant. During dinner, we discussed the rehearsal. My sister, reviewing the performance of a girl about her age who was playing the Virgin Mary, said rather too audibly that the Virgin's breath smelled like the air in an old inner tube. Her brother said to her, "That's not a very Christian thing to say." She replied, "I'm not a Christian, I'm an Episcopalian." We left the restaurant hurriedly, but unharmed.

TEA WITH THE LANDESMANS

Anne and I often went to Chicago's Intercontinental Hotel to hear Judy Roberts, a fine jazz pianist and a crisp, inventive vocalist. When she did "Spring Can Really Hang You Up The Most,"—a jazz standard recorded by Ella Fitzgerald, Sarah Vaughn, Bette Midler, Chris Connor, Barbra Streisand, Jackie Cain, and Irene Kral, among many others—she sometimes told her audience: "This song was written fifty years ago. It sounds like it was written yesterday."

The lyricist on that song, Fran Landesman, was still active when I wrote this. Since 1964, she had lived and worked in London, but she was originally from New York and she wrote "Spring Can Really..." while living in St. Louis in the 1950s. In my youth, I was a semi-regular at the Crystal Palace, an elegant St. Louis saloon owned by the Landesman brothers, Jay and Fred. Jay was, and is, Fran's husband [both now deceased]. On Fran's early songs, the music was composed by Tommy Wolf, the house pianist; in 1956, Wolf recorded an album of songs he wrote with Fran—"I Love You Real," "It Will Only Hurt A Minute," "There are Days When I Don't Think of You at All." Very hip. A couple of years later they wrote the music for *The Nervous Set,* a show originally produced at the Crystal Palace that later had a short run on Broadway, where the cast featured a young Larry Hagman. The original cast recording is still in print. The Crystal Palace production included "Spring Can Really...," but the song was not in the New York show because the owner of the song rights demanded a large fee. People who saw both versions said it was better in St. Louis. Broadway show doctors had made it slick and false.

Judy Roberts urged me to write to Fran Landesman to tell her how much pleasure she had given us. I did. Fran sent a gracious response, noting that she had five gigs coming up: "fortunately they are all in London, am getting on in years." I replied that Anne and I planned to be in London in early February, and said that we would love to come to one of her gigs. As it turned out, one was scheduled for Valentine's Day, the day after we returned to the States, but there were none during our visit. Jay responded by email: "Call us...we live at the Angel [a tube stop], which is 8 Duncan Terrace, Islington. Have tea with us." I followed-up and we were invited to visit them on a Sunday afternoon.

There was a fine, misty rain. Not an enthusiastic rain, but enough to get us wet. I was glad that I had worn gym shoes. (Brits call them "trainers." They got me ejected from the Ritz one night. A haughty young man, looking at my shoes, inquired, "Are you a guest in the hotel, sir?") We knew that 8 Duncan Terrace must be near the beginning, but where did it begin? The Duke of Cambridge pub is at one end—the wrong one, as it turned out.

We walked off a bit of lunch. (Not enough.) I rang the bell and Jay buzzed us in. His voice over the intercom promised that he would be right up. He was on the "lower ground" floor—i.e., the below ground floor. Jay was 86, and it took him a couple of minutes to climb the stairs, but he seemed very fit.

The house was informal, lived in. It did not look like the Crystal Palace. Jay told us that houses in the neighborhood sold for very little when they bought there, when the fashionable place was Chelsea, "on the other side of town," but that Duncan Terrace houses now sold for £1 million. On Friday evening, a prominent barrister had said to us: "Oh, Duncan Terrace. That's a lovely street. Splendid houses there."

At the Landesmans, we sat at a dining table in a ground floor room, overlooking the street. One wall was dominated by a large abstract oil painted by Jay's late brother, Fred. Another had a big etched glass mirror from a pub. The kitchen adjoined at the rear, overlooking a lovely green garden with a rampant vine that invaded the neighbors.

Jay made tea. He poured the water into the pot

from a saucepan, with a steady hand. Impressive. He asked whether we took sugar or milk. Foolishly, we said that we took milk, which necessitated another trip for him on the stairs. *The Camden New Journal,* their neighborhood newspaper, says that Fran lives upstairs and Jay lives downstairs. That seems right. She is quoted: "I married you for better or for worse, but never for lunch."

Fran joined us after a few minutes. Jay had told us that she suffered from macular degeneration. She was, in fact, almost totally blind, but she could still see a bit, well enough to write—not entirely legibly, but well enough. More remarkably, she performed, both her poetry and her songs. She didn't sing in public when she was young, but she did at age 78, and very well. On a new CD devoted entirely to her lyrics, some performed by the likes of Susannah McCorkle and Jamie Cullum, Fran sings "Leopards" and "Down"("There's something irresistible in down"). Her voice and style are reminiscent of Rosemary Clooney at the end of her career, or maybe Walter Huston on "September Song," which is to say that she doesn't have much range but has a great way with a lyric, great feeling for the music, great presence.

After forty-two years in London, neither Fran nor Jay had picked up a British accent. This was surprising because they had good ears. Jay sounded like St. Louis and Fran sounded like a cultivated New

Yorker—not a George Plimpton, which was halfway across the ocean, or a Norman Mailer, which is whatever he chooses at the moment, but the accent of, say, a partner at Sullivan & Cromwell. (A. J. Liebling once said that having Whitey Bimstein as your cut man was like being represented by Sullivan and Cromwell.) I wondered whether Fran and Jay had made an effort to remain American.

We talked a bit about the Iraq war. Fran was very clear that we should not be there. She was wearing a silver ring with the peace symbol. Jay, however, was unwilling to criticize his native land. I provided enough criticism for both of us.

We also talked about the old days in St. Louis, sharing memories of the Crystal Palace, especially the shows. There can be no doubt that Jay had a sharp eye for talent. Before they became truly big names, he booked Mike Nichols and Elaine May, when they were still in the Compass Players in Chicago, Barbra Streisand, Lenny Bruce, Woody Allen. I saw some of them, not all. We also talked about C.P. performers who are less famous: Tom O'Horgan ("and his hip harp"), who went on to direct *Hair;* Will Holt, who did a version of Cole Porter's "I Love Paris" in which it repeatedly became other Porter songs, mostly "Begin the Beguine;"

As we were getting ready to leave, Jay said, playfully, "I'll bet this has been the high point of your trip." I said: "It certainly has. [pause] But, then, we have been hanging out with lawyers and politicians, so don't let it go to your head." Fran applauded.

On our way out the door, Jay said: "You kids have fun!" Since I would be 70 in a few months, that produced a good laugh.

We were scheduled to have dinner at the Connaught that night, our last night in London. We cancelled. The Landesmans were enough rich fare for any one day.

STABILITY

What are we to make of a man who, except when traveling (and he did not travel much), for years ate every Sunday lunch at the same coffee shop and every Friday dinner at a small Mexican American Middle Eastern Ozark cafe? It is true. I did this. And I liked it. Why?

Is it to be attributed to a lack of imagination? Surely not. New restaurants are, in fact, hard to avoid. Was this, then, a form of compulsive behavior, or an unexamined habit, like always putting your pants on right leg first? Not at all. So, again, why?

In the first place, the food was good. The Friday night place provided a bit of culinary surprise, welcome at the end of the work week, and the Sunday place was totally unsurprising, which can also be a very good thing, especially when one is dealing primarily with eggs.

Moreover, the routine provided fixed points by which to navigate. In this uncertain world, we need a bit of predictability. The appeal of variety is vastly overrated. Consider the amount of grief caused, to themselves and to others, by those who seek variety in their sexual partners. Can the pleasure possibly be worth it? It is hard to believe that new lovers, like new restaurants, do not often disappoint.

Does this mean that I am risk averse? Of course. Who in his right mind would not be? Those who constantly seek risk for the sake of risk must be masochists, and possibly self-destructive. No doubt there is no gain unless something is ventured, but I would rather venture some hard work or a bit of time (not too much) than my neck or my livelihood. I will, then, never be wealthy, but I will be comfortable — or, at least have I been so far. T. E. Lawrence is remembered, but he was a very unhappy man. Suffering is only romantic when the other guy does it.

Regularity is desirable. Compounds containing fiber are sold with the representation that they promote it. Now, I will admit that my adherence to these principles may be extreme. When visiting London, for example, I am apt to return to places where I have been before. If I were to go to, perhaps, the Imperial War Museum, I would surely learn something new and it might even be interesting, but this would occupy time that could be spent at the Tate. Would the beer at a new pub be as good? Maybe. But why should one write-off the value of experience? Many hours were invested in research discovering establishments that store their ale properly and ban electronic games. It is now time to harvest the value from that investment.

Devotion does, however, have its costs. The couple who owned the Sunday lunch place retired, and the landlord leased the building to a fast-food chain. Disaster. Then, two months ago, the Friday night place decided to stop serving dinner. It does not have a liquor license, and you can't do much dinner business without one unless you are just a burger joint. The slough of despond.

I am still trying to recover from the dislocation. One of my teachers, John Kautsky, proposed an academic conference addressing the question, "Is Good Change Desirable?" He was prepared to uphold the negative.

Morning, After the Ball

ON IMMORTALITY

Why do people want to be remembered after death? However much they may enjoy attention, it will be hard to take pleasure from it when they are unresponsive in the extreme. Perhaps the mere expectation or possibility of attention is satisfying—the notion that, even when one is no longer around to demand it, obeisance will be paid.

Or maybe the idea is that, so long as something you created survives, a piece of you lives—and the goal is to extend life, symbolically. I've made a couple of canoe paddles, one of walnut and one of cherry, carved with a draw knife and a spokeshave. Walnut and cherry are both pretty durable; the paddles will no doubt survive me, and they are rather handsome objects that could be used with some appreciation after I'm dead. But I don't think I'll find it satisfying to live on as a canoe paddle.

I suppose the point is that endurance is a measure of quality. The concept of "lasting value" has currency despite the long runs of "Cats," Lawrence Welk, and The Incomparable Hildegarde. Indeed, I gather that our most casual and trivial thoughts now live on in cyberspace, whether we wish them to or not. The old saw was "gone but not forgotten." Now it must be "forgotten but not gone."

We like to have other people value our work, of course, especially those whose judgment we respect. Endurance extends that appreciation, and it also implies that the quality of the work transcends fashion. It means not only that your allotment of fame will exceed the fifteen minutes promised by Warhol, but that your stuff was truly good. It rests on faith that Gershwin, Porter, Arlen and Ellington will survive when Lord Lloyd Weber has passed over.

Some people think of their children in this way, which seems dangerous. We should not burden children with the duty to live for the greater glory of their parents, and we should not seek to substitute our children's accomplishments for our own. Their virtues do not belong to us — perhaps their failings do, but not their accomplishments. It is possible to damage children, even to ruin them by being abusive or overly protective, but I don't think one can craft them so as to produce success. At some point, they become willful, and they should.

If you are a teacher, it is well to remember that the same thing is true of students. You can teach them some things, but you cannot justly take credit for their success. Nonetheless, unless the teacher is a truly exceptional scholar, he or she is more likely to be remembered for teaching than for any research or writing. Few academic books are read a decade after they were published, even though many are kept in print far beyond the time when a commercial publisher would have sent them to a landfill. Almost none, apart from textbooks, go into a second edition. Edward Shils thought that scholars should not cite living authors. He was the anti-Warhol.

Tom's Trunk Shop, Gabriels, NY

LEAVING THE HOME PLACE

The house on Main Street is now unoccupied. We will sell it. My brother and sister and their spouses have work elsewhere, and there wouldn't be opportunities for them in Carlinville. My wife and I are, in principle, free to relocate, but it would be foolish for us to move into a large house in our late seventies. None of the next generation—not my children, nor my brother's or sister's—ever lived in Carlinville, and none have reason to be there.

Other large Victorian houses in the neighborhood are on the market, and have been for some time. Few people want them. They are impractical, expensive to heat and maintain, difficult to clean, too large, too gracious. When those houses were built, girls from the farms commonly moved to town to go to high school, and they received room and board in exchange for housework. For several decades now, the girls have come to town on school buses and have gone home in the evening.

But where do they go when they are eighteen? It's a good bet that they don't stay in Carlinville. I left then. I left for the same reasons we all had—to get an education, a job, a spouse, excitement—all good reasons. Still, small town life is attractive. In Carlinville, the Lions Carnival is a real community event. They don't hire a commercial carnival to come to town—instead, the members of the club tend the booths, raffle off cakes, supervise pony rides, and are dunked in a tank of water when a baseball hits the target. It sounds like something out of the 1950s, and it is, but it brings the community together. You see your neighbors, and you recognize them as your neighbors. I once thought that all the talk about rural virtues was pure foolishness; now I'm not so sure. This may be an old man's romantic notion, a view from a distance, both geographic and temporal, but I feel we have lost something.

In her sixties, Gertrude Stein famously said that she did not feel a connection to Oakland, where she had spent her youth—"there is no there there." In contrast, Edmund Wilson, no fan of Stein, took up residence in his later years in an old stone house in upstate New York where his ancestors had lived and where he summered as a boy.

He said that he felt "quite at home" there, that he belonged, and that he was not treated as a stranger, as he was in New England.

I sometimes feel much that way about Carlinville, but it is no longer true that I know everybody. I've now been gone longer than Edmund Wilson was away from Talcottville, and many of the people I knew have moved away or died. Still, I'm not exactly a foreigner. I have relatives in Carlinville and I occasionally meet acquaintances at the grocery store. But I've lived elsewhere for sixty years.

Many of the noteworthy furnishings of the Main Street house — Major Burke's bed, the needlepoint portrait of Saint Patrick, the big secretary — are massive and ornate, and Anne and I lack the vision required to fit them into modern décor. Why does this bother me? My life and the lives of my children and grandchildren will not really change if the family heritage is sold. Putting it in those terms, of course, is tendentious. Are we really selling the heritage? The furniture, the paintings, and the house where the family lived for nearly a century are only things, after all. What will we lose?

I think the answer is that family heirlooms reinforce our sense of who we are. A part of our identity is in them. This has something to do, I suppose, with the power of early memories, but my early memories are, usually, not especially dramatic or important. Nothing traumatic or even exceptional happened. Although I lived through World War II, I was very young and the only parts I really recall are the celebration of victory and the joyful return of our troops. I do remember lying on the floor of the living room when the Main Street house was occupied by my grandparents, drawing pictures and copying the portrait of Major Burke while my grandfather listened to the radio. This was the room in which he wept when he heard about the Bank Holiday. In the dining room, I sat through innumerable family meals and heard accounts of Macoupin history and the family's part in it. The drawer that held my crayons—in a long, narrow table made of oak in the Arts and Crafts style, fumed to resemble ebony—is still there. The drawer still smells of crayons, and I remember the drawings and my grandparents' encouragement. The house is full of people once close to me.

Will strangers who buy the house understand what to do with it, how to live in it? What will they make of a parlor and a living room, next to each other? My grandfather and grandmother would not object to using the space as a library or even a billiard room, but an electronic entertainment center would be out of place. Will the new owners paint the woodwork, lightening the interior but obscuring the quarter-sawn oak? Will they replace the window frames so that standardized storm windows will fit? If they get rid of the old furniture, as they surely must, will the presence of my parents and grandparents still be felt in the rooms? If I'm not there to sense that presence, does it matter? At some point while we still own the house, I will make a final visit. Perhaps, during that visit, I'll see my tweed cap on the sideboard near the front door and then remember my grandmother saying that a hat can look like a man. The new owners will hear their own voices in those rooms and, in time, find their own memories there. For now, my father's singing, laughter at the dinner table, and my children's first words can still be summoned. When the house goes, I'll lose some of the triggers of memory.

It is hard to escape the attraction, the pull, the idea that there is a home place. Some people, although fewer now than formerly, identify with a house or a town. When Edmund Wilson inherited the stone house, he found it "moldy-smelling" and "rubbishy," but he resolved to "preserve it, make it something my own." He observed that our ancestors moved "farther and farther West," motivated by the desire for new lives. Carlinville was one of the farther places. Major Burke came from Virginia, Peter Heinz from Germany, and Peter Denby from Yorkshire, but they all struggled to make lives in the wilderness, and I could still see the struggle when I was in high school. I'm not sure that I can today. Perhaps if I were writing this in Carlinville, I might. The tower of the Main Street house, at the front of the second floor, has a room that is an excellent place to write. My grandfather had a big rolltop desk there.

WALKING FREE

In the 1960s, all Northwestern law professors had bronze nameplates on their office doors. Bronze! Cast, not painted. Faculty did not often move from school to school in those days. The plates were a foot or more in length, depending upon the number of letters in the name. The honorific was "Mr. or "Mrs.," not "Prof.," and certainly not "Dr." even though the J. D. degree had replaced the traditional LL.B. at most schools. We were lawyers. I still have the bronze "Mr. Heinz" in my basement (along with much else).

A few months after my 70th birthday, I received from Northwestern a letter informing me that tenured faculty age 65 and older were being offered a generous financial incentive to waive their tenure rights and retire promptly. After forty-two years as a professor, this had a certain appeal. The recent death of a colleague had made me the senior member of the faculty, but that was an honor roughly equivalent to inheriting the family cakestand.

I found the prospect of retirement troubling. Did I have enough ideas to fill my days? I don't golf, I don't schmooze comfortably, and I don't like to sit unless I have a sitting-down-task. Perhaps, I thought, retirement would be like wandering around London. The Air Force had once deposited me in London for several days while people with business did it. I simply walked around. I explored an endless succession of bookstores, pubs, curiosity shops, Sir John Soane's house in Lincoln's Inn Fields, the Photographer's Gallery, the Temple Church, places where you could then buy Regency period boxing prints for a couple of pounds and hand-colored bookplates by the Cruikshanks for even less. My legs were sore but I was happy. I thought a good retirement might be much the same.

Being seventy struck me as odd. My father didn't reach that age. But, in truth, I had thought I might get there. I didn't know of anything that was going to kill me, soon. I was becoming deaf, but that can be a blessing, and my knees, which had ached a few years before, actually seemed better. Most of the plumbing still worked.

None of my previous birthdays had impressed anyone. This one did. Strangers handed a piece of identification remarked on my great age. They could sometimes be persuaded to marvel at how young I looked. All in all, it was fun to be an authentic relic yet still moving. I found that I could impress law students simply by jumping rope—not well, but at all.

To celebrate the birthday, Anne and I went to

dinner at the Wawbeek, a relic of even greater antiquity. It was an inn in the Adirondacks, on the shore of Upper Saranac Lake, and it had been there (or nearby, allowing for the effects of a few fires) for a century. The two of us dined upstairs on the screened porch overlooking the lake, with a view of the High Peaks in the distance. It was a fine August night. The food was good, the claret was excellent, and the company could not have been better. The Wawbeek is now gone, regrettably. The property was bought, and the inn demolished, by the creator of the Eveready bunny advertisements. But we are still marching.

A book and several articles have been published since I retired. It will be understandable if you haven't noticed. There are those of my fellows who suggest that I should now, at long last, be quiet. There is certainly something to be said for that option. I would, however, like to think that I might still produce some good work. In *Beyond the Fringe* a man impatient for the end of the world says "there must be a winner one day".

But I found the prospect of retirement challenging. Might I occupy my time writing essays? Perhaps. I knew there's no audience for such work, of course. Writing essays is a bit like singing to an empty theater. Without bodies to absorb the sound, you hear the echo of your own voice.

I located a drawer large enough to hold the essays, resting comfortably. My fantasy was that they would be discovered in time to be reproduced on an old-fashioned mimeograph machine and distributed to the guests at my funeral, who would then get the ink on their hands, giving them something to remember me by.

Adirondack Knitter, Coreys

ACKNOWLEDGMENTS

I'm grateful to the mysterious, masked model who appears in four of the pictures. I have a relationship with her that I like to think of as similar to the relationship that Man Ray had with Kiki de Montparnasse.

A friend of very long standing, Harvey Wilcox, read many of these essays in an earlier attempt at compilation. He is an excellent editor and he made many helpful notes, including telling me to ditch some stuff. He was right. He also suggested that I might package this as a walk around Carlinville, with memories triggered by places seen along the way. Harv could probably have pulled that off. I could not.

The late Alfred Appel, an author, wit, frequent lunch companion, and dear friend told me about his writing and I told him about mine. It is impossible to catalog the ideas I got from Alfred, but there were many. I miss him.

Anne Godden-Segard, a Brit, is another writer and

friend of long standing. We worked together several years ago at the American Bar Foundation, and she saw many of these essays in early drafts. She told me which ones were good and which ones to discard.

I'm grateful to Carole Mabus and Irv Slate for similar evaluations. They read the essays, criticized the ones that were weak, and identified those that were favorites. It's difficult to find people who are willing and able to provide that service—it takes time and requires critical judgment. They are true friends.

William Conger, a prominent Chicago artist whose paintings graced the covers of two of my novels, was a colleague of mine at Northwestern. He was the chairman of the university's department of Art Theory and Practice. We collaborate constantly, exchanging ideas and complaints. He has been to Carlinville and stayed at the Main Street House.

During the last stages of editing, I asked Walt Harrington, a distinguished writer and editor, to read the manuscript. He kindly and generously agreed. (I think the fact that I was from Carlinville had something to do with it.) He saw that one of the essays lacked detail, and I acted on that. If you want to know how to do this work, read Harrington's *Artful Journalism* (2018).

Evan Meagher advised me during the later stages of the work on the manuscript. He was one of the best students I ever had during 42 years of teaching at Northwestern Law School. During his first weeks there, he was still a professional baseball player in France on the weekends—a long-ball hitter. In addition to being a firstrate lawyer and the former chief financial officer of a tech company, he plays very good jazz harmonica. I was fortunate to have the benefit of his counsel. He is also a good writer—see his *Have Bat, Will Travel.*

J. H.
April, 2025

Sunset at Coreys

INDEX

Abraham Lincoln Brigage, 26
Adirondacks, 3, 76, 147
Ahab, Captain, 2, 42
Air Force, U. S., 29-31, 36, 49, 102, 146
Algonquins, 76
Ali, Muhammad, 83, 85
Allen, Woody, 83, 84, 130
American Bar Foundation, 151
Amtrak, 23, 124
Anchor Inn, Carlinville, 117
Angus Bailey's Steak House, Carlinville, 25
Appel, Alfred, 77, 150
Arlen, Harold, 137
Artful Journalism, 151
Arts and Crafts style, 143
Atlantic, The, 83
Auteuil Races, 15

Bacall, Lauren, 52, 84
Baines, Mr. and Mrs. Huffman, 49-50
Bank Holiday, 60, 143
Banville, John, 96
Baptist Church, 71
Barnes & Noble, 2
Bear Rough School, 16
Begin the Beguine (song), 130

Belafonte, Harry, 75
Between Meals, 96
Beyond the Fringe, 147
Bimstein, Whitey, 130
Black, Benjamin, 96
Blackburn College, Carlinville, 88
Blair House, 51
Blair, Eric, 96
Blue house farm, 5, 55, 61
Boente, Dana, 124
Boente's Shell Station, 124
Bois de Boulogne, 15
Boy Scouts, 9
Boyle, Peter, 49
Broadway, 127
Brown, Dan, 2
Bruce, Lenny, 130
Burke family, 107
Burke, Beatty T., 106-109, 122, 142-144
Burke, Don Alonzo, 106
Burke, Tennessee (Tennie), 108
Byron, Lord, 78, 106

Cain, Jackie, 126
Camden New Journal, The, 129
Carlin-villa Motel, Carlinville, 25
Carlinville, Illinois, 12, 16, 22, 25, 29, 40, 44, 50, 87, 109-110, 113, 115-116, 140-144, 150-151
Carnegie Hall Concert, 1938, 20
Cassidy, Hopalong, 8
Catholics, 72, 119
Cats, 136

Census, U. S. 1870, 12
Central West End, St. Louis, 110
Cheerios, 92
Chekhov, Anton, 14
Chicago, 19, 25, 36, 84, 113, 134
Chicago and Alton Railroad, 16
Christmas, 12, 71
Clemens, Samuel, 96
Clooney, Rosemary, 129
Coakley, Bill, 54
Cobb, Lee J., 52
College Inn, nightclub, 20
Compass Players (Chicago), 130
Conger, William, 151
Connaught Hotel, London, 131
Connor, Chris, 126
Crack-Up, The, 52
Cruikshanks (George and Isaac Robert), 146
Crystal Palace, 126-130
Cuban Missile Crisis, 31
Cullum, Jamie, 129
Culver Military Academy, 9-11
Cunningham, Joe, 110
Curious Case of Sid Finch, The, 80
Cushman motor scooter, 123

Dada, 53
de Kooning, Willem, 80
de Montparnasse, Kiki, 3, 53, 150
Dean, James, 14
Death of a Salesman, 52
Dee, Jonathan, 84

Democratic National Convention, 1968, Chicago, 36
Dempsey, Jack, 77
Denby family, 6, 19, 44
Denby, Dr. John P. (grandfather), 5, 6, 60, 61, 68, 118, 143
Denby, Helen Burke (maternal grandmother), 108, 143
Denby, Peter (great-grandfather), 144
Dictionary of American Slang, 88
Donleavy, J. P., 94-98
Down (song), 129
Drosten's Restaurant, Carlinville, 87-88, 115
Dublin, Ireland, 94
Dunnock, Mildred, 52

Earl of Louisiana, The, 62, 96
Egan, Pierce, 42
Elaine's Restaurant, New York, 82
Ellington, Duke, 52, 137
Episcopal Church, Carlinville, 70, 71, 125
Evanston Public Library, 94, 98
Evanston, Illinois, 22

Fagerquist, Don, 20
Farmers' and Merchants' Bank, 61
Federal Bureau of Investigation (FBI), 100-102
Festival of the Arts, White House, 52-54
Fite, Scrappy, 50
Fitzgerald, Ella, 126
Fitzgerald, F. Scott, 52
Fitzsimmons, Bob, 62
Florida, 16
Fornero, Sheik, 117
Fowles, John, 43

Frankenthaler, Helen, 80

Gallico, Paul, 77
Gaslight Square, 110-111
Gatsby, Jay, 2
George IV, 78
German Patriots (Schurz, Hecker), 109
Gershwin, George, 137
Gershwin, Ira, 137
Ginger Man, The, 94
Glades, The, restaurant, Carlinville, 25, 117
Godden-Segard, Anne, 150
Goldwater, Barry, 102
Goodman, Benny, 20
Grant, Cary, 8, 52
Guardian, The, 94
Gulf, Mobile & Ohio Railroad, 124

Hagman, Larry, 127
Hair, 130
Halberstam, David, 83
Hampton Court, 81
Harrington, Walt, 151
Hasselblad, 3
Have Bat, Will Travel, 152
Hayward, Wisconsin, 113
Heinz, Anne, 126, 127, 150
Heinz, family, 16
Heinz, Furniture Store, Carlinville, 118
Heinz, Gustav (grandfather), 118
Heinz, Harold (uncle), 12
Heinz, Hotel, 117

Heinz, Peter (great-grandfather), 109, 144
Heinz, Peter (son), 22
Heinz, William H. (father), 12
Heller, Joseph, 95
Henry VIII, 81
Hersey, John, 53
Hildegarde, The Incomparable, 136
Hiroshima, 53
History of Macoupin County, 1879, 70, 106, 109
Hodges, Johnny, 52
Hollywood, 8
Holt, Will, 130
Howards of Virginia, The, 8
Hudson's Bay Company, 76
Huston, Walter, 129

I Love Paris (song), 130
I Love You Real (song), 126
Ibbetson house, 55
Illinois Terminal System (ITS), 110
Imperial War Museum, 133
In Defense of the Sweet Science, 41
Indian Carry, 76
Intercontinental Hotel, Chicago, 126
Ireland, 66, 94, 98
It will Only Hurt a Minute (song), 126

Jackson, John, 78-79
Jenkins, Walter, 102
Johnson, Lyndon, 49, 102

Kautsky, John, 134

Kennedy, Robert, 36
Kevlar, 75
King, Martin Luther, Jr., 36
Klee, Paul, 2
Kosinski, Jerzey, 84
Kral, Irene, 126
Krupa, Gene, 19-21

Lake Shore Drive, Chicago, 24
Landesman, Fran and Jay, 126-131
Landesman, Fred, 126
Lartigue, Jacques Henri, 15
Lartigue, Zissou, 15
Lawrence, T. E., 133
Leopards (song), 129
Liberace, 96
Liebling, A. J., 2, 42, 62, 96, 130
Life Magazine, 24
Lincoln's Inn Fields, 146
Linonia & Brothers room, Yale Library, 42
Lions Carnival, 141
Lloyd Weber, Andrew, 137
Loges family, 14, 15
Loges, Bernadine, 14-16
London, 126, 146
Lowell, Robert, 53
Lowther, Hugh, Earl Lonsdale, 78, 79
Lutheran Church, 70

Mabus, Carole, 151
Macoupin Club, 16-17
Macoupin County, 23, 28, 44, 57

Magnolia's restaurant, Carlinville, 25
Mailer, Norman, 79, 83, 130
Main Street House, Carlinville, 64, 67, 106-107, 140, 151
Malcolm X, 36
Man Ray, 3, 52, 53, 150
Marvel Theater, 8, 88
May, Elaine, 130
McCarthy, Joseph, 103
McCorkle, Susannah, 129
McDonald, Dwight, 53
McQueen, Steve, 39
Meagher, Evan, xiii-xv, 152
Memoirs of a Revolutionist, 53
Messick house, 55
Middle West, 97
Midler, Bette, 126
Miller, Lee, 53
Mineo, Sal, 20
Minton house, Carlinville, 55
Moore, Archie, 42, 77
Moore, Davey, 41
Morse family, 123
Mulligan, Gerry, 20

Napoleon III, 106
Nativity pageant, 125
Nervous Set, The, 127
New York Review of Books, 53
New Yorker, The, 55, 94, 96
Nichols, Mike, 130
Nick's Pizza, Carlinville, 25
North By Northwest, 52

Northwestern Law School, xiii-xv, 145, 152
Northwestern University, 80, 145, 151

O'Brien, Philadelphia Jack, 62
O'Hara, John, 82
O'Horgan, Tom, 130
O'Neill, Eugene, 14
Oakland, California, 141
Occidental restaurant, D. C., 32
Onassis, Jacqueline Kennedy, 84
Opper's strawberry farm, 123
Orwell, George, 96

Paret, Benny, 41
Paris Review, The, 80
Parker, Charlie, 20
Pentagon, 30, 31, 36, 47, 53-54, 100
People magazine, 85
Photographers' Gallery, London, 146
Plimpton, George, 77, 80-85, 130
Porter, Cole, 130, 137
Prairie Farms Creamery, Carlinville, 23
Presbyterian Church, 71
Prince Regent, 78
Puttin' On the Ritz (song), 49

Queensberry Rules, 79

Racquet Club, New York, 81
Rayburn, Sam, 31
Regency period, 78, 146
Regional Transit Authority, 57

Reno's Pizza, Carlinville, 25
Roadfood, 115, 120
Robards, Jason, 52
Roberts, Judy, 126, 127
Robinson vs. California, xiv, 33
Rodney, Red, 20
Roosevelt, Frankin Delano, 60
Roper's Dairy Bar, Carlinville, 115
Rosolino, Frank, 20
Royalex, 75

Saints Mary and St. Joseph, Carlinville, 72
Saturday Night Live, 83
Scali, John, 32
Schlessinger, Arthur, Jr., 52
Schoendienst, Red, 97
Selma March, 36
Selvo, Jerk, 117
September Song (song), 129
Shadow Box, 79, 83
Shavers, Ernie, 85
Sheraton Hotels, 84
Sherman Hotel, Chicago, 20
Shils, Edward, 138
Sing Sing Sing (song), 20
Singular Country, A, 94, 98
Slate, Irv, 151
Slaughter, Enos, 97
Smokey Joe's Grecian Terrace, 110
Soane, Sir John, 146
Southern Baptists, 72
Speedos, 113

Spofford, Harriet, 83
Sports Illustrated, 42, 77
Spot, The, restaurant, 125
Spring Can Really Hang You Up the Most (song), 126
St. John, Jill, 52
St. Lawrence River, 76
St. Louis World's Fair, 1904, 116
St. Louis, Missouri, 66, 108, 110, 126-130
St. Patrick, 66
St. Regis Hotel, New York, 84
Steichen, Edward, 52
Stein, Gertrude, 141
Stern, Jane and Michael, 115
Stony Creek Ponds, 76
Streisand, Barbra, 126, 130
Sullivan & Cromwell, 130
Sullivan, John L., 78
Supreme Court, U. S., 33
Sweet Science, The, 41, 42, 62, 96

Talese, Gay, 83
Tate Museum, 133
Taylor, Charles O., 116
Taylor's Chili Parlor, Carlinville, 25, 115-120
Temple Church, London, 146
Tender is the Night, 52
There are Days When I Don't Think of You at All (song), 126
Toynbee, Arnold, 62
Trinity College, Dublin, 94
Twain, Mark, 96

Union League Club, 42

University of Chicago, 80
Upjohn's Rural Architecture, 70
Upper Saranac Lake, 147

Valley Forge, 8, 9
Vaughn, Sarah, 126
Vietnam War, xiii, 29, 36, 53-54

Wales, 3
Walmart, 24, 72, 122
Warhol, Andy, 80, 137
Washington University, 110
Wawbeek, The, 147
Welk, Lawrence, 136
Wentworth, Harold, 88
West Main Street, 23, 117
White House, 47, 101-102
White, E. B., 2
Wilcox, Harvey, 150
Wilde, Oscar, 79
Wildroot Cream Oil, 88
Wilroy, Mary Edith, 51
Wilson, Edmund, 141, 144
Wolf, Tommy, 126
Wood, Grant, 124
World War II, 8, 24, 45, 55, 75, 94, 142

Yale Law School, 29
YMCA (Washington, D.C.), 102
YMCA (Wisconsin), 113
Young Frankenstein, 49

www.ingramcontent.com/pod-product-compliance
Lightning Source LLC
Chambersburg PA
CBHW042138160426
43200CB00020B/2974